Groping Toward Whatever

OR

How I Learned To Retire

[SORT OF]

Groping Toward Whatever

OR

How I Learned To Retire

[SORT OF]

SUSAN TRAUSCH

FREE STREET PRESS

Published by
Free Street Press
131 Free Street
Hingham, MA 02043

www.freestreetpress.com

Editor: Sharon Cloud Hogan
Cover, Typesetting, and Interior Design: Janis Owens, Books By Design, Inc.

ISBN: 978-0-9828136-9-0

Library of Congress Control Number: 2010930701

PRINTED IN THE UNITED STATES OF AMERICA

For John

Contents

✳

Groping Toward Whatever

OR

How I Learned To Retire

[SORT OF]

CHAPTER 1

Who Am I?

The experts tell you to have a retirement plan, to know where you're going before you're out the office door and gone. I didn't have a clue when I left the *Boston Globe* in December 2005 with a severance package and 32 years of newspaper clips. I just bolted and groped.

I'm still groping. It's not a bad way to live, but it requires yoga. It requires practice, this shedding of the career skin, this letting go of what *was* to figure out what *is*, and what might be. It requires patience, this loss of control, this chucking of the 9-to-5 schedule, ditching of deadline demand that ticked like an atomic clock in the brain and kept time with a fractured mantra of Descartes: *I'm published therefore I am.*

Not getting published means what exactly? I'm learning what, and not so exactly. I'm learning that transitions, no matter how easy they seem in the abstract or how exhilarating they feel as the door opens wide to freedom, are never simple. Human beings are contradictory little devils with egos that can bite them in the butt on a morning when everything seems perfect.

"You need business cards," the woman on the phone said. She was being helpful and friendly, but her words zinged right under my skin. She'd been a book publicist for years and had lots of cards. I'd been retired less than a week and had a few old ones that said "Editorial Writer." I'd called her to ask if she'd talk to a young friend who was new in town and wanted to get into publishing. This was not supposed to be about me. I needed no help being deliriously happy at home in my bathrobe without portfolio at 10:30 in the morning.

"Cards? You're kidding."

"To keep your name in circulation," she explained. "To have something to hand out to people so they'll know where to reach you."

"What if they don't want to reach me?"

"Assume they do."

"What do I call myself on this card?"

"You don't call yourself anything. Just print your name, address, phone number, and e-mail."

"That's it? People aren't going to say, 'You forgot something at the printer?' They're not going to think, 'What's the point if she's not starting her own company, teaching, joining a public relations firm, or preparing for a backpacking trip in Katmandu?'"

"It's a calling card, okay?"

A calling card on which there was nothing to call myself? A calling card, like something out of a Jane Austen novel? Was I supposed to hand them to Beacon Hill doormen to be placed on antique silver trays in wood-paneled foyers? Maybe I was supposed to get my own silver tray and hold it out to passersby on Newbury Street, or hit the intermission crowd at Symphony Hall: "In case you're looking for a fill-in-the-blank, Sir or Madam."

I'd always laughed at cards and titles. My idea of networking was waving to the neighbors on the way into the garage. Of course, I'd always had an identity, had one since age 20, anyway, with the first newspaper job as a summer intern for the *Cleveland Press*. What did I need with fussy cards? The stack of long, narrow, brown reporter's notebooks in the desk told people who I was. The *desk* told them, and the phone with the same extension for three decades, and the byline. I belonged to a masthead, a big room with presses that shook a building, a fleet of trucks, a Constitutional power that legitimized a nervous voice on the phone. I was the working press. It said so on the press pass.

And now? Should that pass say "Retired Press," "Journalist Emeritus?" Nothing?

I didn't order the calling cards. But was that because the idea was truly silly or because the ego refused to hang out there alone in too much white space without a label? The truth was somewhere not quite in the middle. At age 60, despite a career, I felt professionally naked with nary a fig leaf to cover the question Americans ask each other in the same breath with "Hello": *What do you DO?*

Saying "I'm retired" wasn't DOING. Saying "I write fiction" sounded as though the stuff was selling. Saying, "I do water aerobics three times a week and walk the other days and pull weeds in the middle of a summer morning and feel fabulously alive even when I'm confused" was way too long and lacked gravitas.

"My 80-year-old mother does water aerobics," said the husband of a friend. His mother was in an assisted living facility.

"You need a catch-all phrase, something short that defines your work," said John, my husband. "Tell them you're working on a book."

Was I? "Working on a book" sounded so concrete, so "first draft on a disk, agent on the phone."

How about being a consultant? Wasn't everyone? But a consultant to whom about what? In writing groups I introduced myself as a "recovering journalist," which didn't sound right for general public consumption.

"I'm a writer" was true enough, but it had the whiff of pomposity and begged more probing questions such as, "Where have you been published?"

"Nowhere now" sounded so sad, and "I gave up steady publication and a paycheck to collect rejection slips from obscure literary journals" sounded like an old Bob Newhart joke. Doing a telephone monologue as Abe Lincoln's harried press agent, Newhart would say, "No, no, Abe. First you were a rail splitter, THEN an attorney."

Was I crazy? Yes. Would I go back to the old job? No. Ambiguity was better than certainty in an office with no air. Confusion and contradiction were better than feeling dried up physically and creatively. It was long past time to bolt — not from editorial-page colleagues and editors, who were the best anyone could have — but from an industry that seemed to be dying. Mostly I had to bolt because of the deadness I felt in myself.

On good days, I knew that. On bad days, I'd get rattled by something as routine as the town census form that came in the mail and listed me a "reporter." I didn't change it. I didn't know what to change it to. And when the federal income-tax form listed me as "journalist," I left it and didn't type in "recovering."

On good days, I was the bold philosophical seeker going out on the great adventure, unconcerned with what anyone thought. Popeye facing the ocean gale, bellowing, "I am what I am!"

On bad days, I wanted to hug the manager of a wine store who looked at my credit card and said, "I know that name. Didn't you write for the *Boston Globe?*" YES! YES! I am what I *was*! And would you please announce it over the store's public address system?

Pathetic. And even more pathetic was hoping managers and clerks in other stores would notice the name on the card, especially if they had gray hair and looked as though they remembered life before the Internet.

Pathetic was hoping the plumber might remember that I used to be somebody. He didn't. And he didn't care that the reason I was home in the afternoon on a weekday was that I'd retired after 32 long years. I'd drop that into conversations, the 32 long years at the *Boston Globe*. It was important. It was validation, a way of saying I'd worked hard at something interesting, punched the clock, done the tour, had a life.

Was I boring now? Losing the fastball? Forgetting how to run for a taxi in stacked heels? Was I flunking retirement? Sometimes, yes. But only when I thought I was being graded.

CHAPTER 2

They Paid Me to Leave

I was ready to take the money and run. A lot of us were. We'd been following buyout rumors since the first one became reality in 1992, following them the way railbirds chew up chatter at the track.

"Whaddaya hear?"

"Buyout coming."

"Good one?"

"That's the word."

"Going?"

"Maybe. You?"

"That depends."

"On?"

"The numbers."

"Right. Have to see the offer."

"Has to be worth our while to go."

"No use talking 'til they mail us the numbers."

"Yep. Drive ourselves crazy trying to guess."

"Got that right."

"So, whaddaya hear on the numbers?"

And in the weeks after rumor turned to fact and offers were mailed out, the railbirds stood around comparing lists of potential takers, figuring the odds on who might or might not become a voluntary workforce reduction. Office productivity often goes to hell after a company announces a move to save money.

"I hear *she's* taking it."

"No way! Who else?"

"*Him.*"

"*Him?*"

"Outtaheah! First one to sign."

"Is you-know-who going? Oh please God!"

"Never. Loves torturing us too much."

"Damn. Let's take up a collection, throw in a week at somebody's time-share."

"What about *them?*"

"Iffy. Talking to their accountants. Have to downsize to make it work."

"Worth it."

"Freedom."

"Yeah, baby. Freedom."

We could afford to talk that way. The economy was relatively good — at least it wasn't as bad as it would get in a couple of years — and the *New York Times,* owner of the *Boston Globe,* was not yet threatening to shut the place down. Freedom was a fantasy unencumbered by financial reality. It was a big silver bus, a dream on wheels that would stop outside the building, doors wide open. Destination: Anywhere You Want To Go.

A couple of buses had come and gone in the past decade. I watched people board, waved good-bye, and felt as if friends were heading off to camp while I was in summer school. But "the numbers" weren't good for me — not enough years in, not enough money saved, and maybe I wasn't quite done with the business.

By 2005 I was. When the fat, white, 8- x 10-inch envelopes were mailed to employees' homes, solidifying the speculation with details of a severance package, I was a month away from turning 60 and felt like I'd been handed the perfect birthday present — a bus ticket.

I was euphoric. Except when I wasn't — except when I felt weird.

Weird? Is that the right word? Was I having doubts? No, not doubts, more like regret, nostalgia for what used to be and could not be again, a certain sadness for the good-byes that had to be said to people who shared what felt like a marriage. I was getting divorced, amicably but irrevocably, and divorce is never simple.

Maybe I had a case of nerves, too, feeling the old Wow/ Ow response the way I did leaving Cleveland after college to live in New York City. "Wow!" filled the heart at the sight of the Manhattan skyline, the sense of possibility, and independence. But a persistent little "Ow!" squeaked in the mind's ear when a taxi driver pitched the suitcases into his trunk as though they were garbage, when a piece of dirt flew into my eye, the traffic screamed, and the dingy room with the metal furniture at the Studio Club (a YWCA residence for women in the arts) seemed to sneer: "Go home, Hick. You don't have the guts."

Was I scared to make a megamove at 60 the way I'd been at 21? Scared of leaving home? That's what the *Globe* had been for 32 years — my professional home. But it was so past time to go. I'd signed the papers, let the rescind deadline pass, and was breaking down the office bit by bit, walking out with the old pole lamp, the files, the books, the photos. I was seeing life's skyline, sensing the possibility, tasting the independence, and stuffing insecurity into a carton to deal with later — unless somebody kicked it loose on the way to the parking lot.

"And you'll do what, exactly?" the columnist demanded, standing in the middle of the hall, arms folded across his chest. He'd retired years ago, but he still came in as a freelancer. His bristly white eyebrows moved up and down in an impish, slightly mocking expression. He liked to yank people's chains, but was only half-kidding.

"Don't know yet," I said, concentrating on looking relaxed.

"Don't know?" he persisted. "Don't have a plan?"

"I thought I'd just kind of, you know, hang out for awhile."

His blue eyes narrowed. "Hang out?"

"Until I come up with something."

"Sounds sketchy."

"I'm retiring. Taking a breather. Stopping. For awhile."

"Hmph."

Was stopping not allowed in American culture? How about floundering for awhile and not having an answer? Many colleagues who left that year were similarly vague on plans. Hadn't we earned a break?

A friend who worked for another paper nodded enthusiastically and agreed that I had earned it. But after the high-fives and hugs, she said — almost as an afterthought — "Of course, I would never leave a job unless I had another one."

A retired photographer, who spent as much time continuing to do his old job as the freelancing columnist did, put a brotherly hand on my shoulder in the cafeteria line. "You're going to be all right, Sue," he said, just above a whisper. "Really. You'll be fine."

Was my psychic slip showing? Was there something he knew that was going to keep me awake nights? I would have enjoyed lunch more if he hadn't told me I'd be fine.

"Are you okay?" a 30-something reporter asked as we stood at the sinks in the ladies' room. She asked gently, not wanting to be intrusive. She watched my eyes with the same worried look that had been on the faces of a couple of people I met at church and in the supermarket. The look was partly curiosity. A retired person, or one about to retire, is an exotic, an experiment in life's petri dish. Working people want to get close enough to poke, analyze, and see just how odd the specimen is. The other part of the look was embarrassment and confusion about not knowing what to say because they figured I'd just been handed the journalistic towel.

I had.

It was a really nice towel. Monogrammed. A gift to anyone with the seniority to take it. The towel came with a pension and health benefits. I liked this towel A LOT, and I was lucky to hold it in my ink-stained fingers. Many people weren't so lucky. They were being outsourced, canned, downsized, and sold at newspapers all over the country. A business built around a paper product was being savaged by a new medium — the Internet — and either had to reinvent itself in an electronic age or become extinct.

The world had changed so fast. Packing up boxes in those last days at the paper, I felt as though I were looking at three decades at once, seeing myself at 28 — a reporter flying free on a job that did not feel like work — and at 60, a tired veteran who just wanted out.

Like many veterans leaving other companies in other industries, I had felt the earthquake in corporate culture that occurs when a place is sold, as the *Globe* was to the *Times* in 1993. I took it personally when "my" newspaper was no longer run by the Taylor family, which had been in charge since 1873, and when the chilly corporate types moved in with PowerPoint slides and Harvard Business School-speak, telling reporters to produce "content of transcendent impact" instead of "a damn good read."

I remembered too well the place known as a "writer's paper," which had happily run my business-humor columns that had blown up bureaucratic blah-blah. I could see the late editor-in-chief, Tom Winship, in his red suspenders, tossing me an illegible note scrawled on a paper napkin and yelling over his shoulder, "Call that guy. Helluva story. You'll have fun." No focus group needed. It was a business run by the gut. It was loaded with oddballs and poets, laughter and love, and it was gone.

I felt like Hildy Johnson in a *Dilbert* strip. Where were the typewriters? Who unplugged the wire machines? How did my industry go from being indispensable to being just one more content provider bobbing on the wild informational sea?

"Are you okay?" the young reporter in the ladies' room asked again.

"Totally," I said, my voice sounding hollow as it echoed off the sinks and walls — the walls that needed paint, just as the floor needed scrubbing — details that the Taylors never let slide. But this young reporter had not known the Taylors, or Winship, or life before Wall Street, or me.

"That's good," she said tentatively. I would not have been convinced at her age either, loaded with early career energy and facing an old-timer. I hoped she would grow with the changes and be part of the new newspaper, however it evolved.

"I'm euphoric, even," I continued, thinking that if anyone had handed my younger self a severance package, it would have felt like failure. Now it was a gift.

And yet . . . what? Did I want somebody from corporate to fly in from New York and beg me not to leave? "No, no. We didn't mean *you.*" Does someone who is about to retire always hope for the magic bullet that will bring back youth and the hotshot who was going places in a business that had seemed as vital as water?

The retiring autoworker who watched the industry implode, the textile and shoe manufacturers who saw their skills go south, the mom-and-pop grocery-store owners squeezed out by the supermarkets, and the Polaroid workers who lost pensions from what had been one of the most innovative and socially responsible corporations in America all most likely wanted the good days back for more compelling reasons than my own.

I was okay. I was lucky. I'd been rewarded for the hard work. But on my last day, driving through the *Boston Globe* parking lot, passing the green and gold newspaper trucks parked in rows like sentries guarding the past, I pulled over and cried.

CHAPTER 3

Money and Mortality

After listening to the accountant, the investment manager, and the financial planner, I was sure of just one thing: retirement is a crapshoot.

And that was back in the relatively giddy days of '05 and '06 when mortgage bankers were still handing out money to people who didn't have jobs. That was before the market blew up and the economy dropped down the dumper. Had I known the market would blow up and the economy would drop down the dumper I would have kept working. But the accountant, the investment manager, and the financial planner didn't have that information. They are in the business of generalities, scenarios, projections, and spreadsheets. And a person who is about to retire wants it all, and he or she pays money to sit down with these people to go over page after page of vague, confusing computer printouts that may, or may not, have much to do with reality.

The exercise is called "running the numbers," which sounds faintly illicit and as though the computers might be sitting in a back room at the corner gas station. Or they could be sitting in a corral in some fiduciary Pamplona, waiting for the gates to be flung open for a mathematical running of the bulls — which in many ways this is. And the really crazy-making part is being responsible for providing the numbers that will be run by the experts with the computers. I spent days digging utility bills and insurance premiums out of drawers, trolling through the checkbook and crumpled grocery-store receipts, and pressing the memory to come up with more than a loose tally of some, but not all, Dunkin' Donuts drive-thru stops and impulse purchases at the bookstore. Does one count greeting cards? How many a month? Are the Girl Scout cookies a charity donation or food? Could the "miscellaneous" category possibly be adding up to half the mortgage?

The expense total, accurate or not, would become the monthly outgo that would be subtracted from the monthly income, adjusted for inflation, and projected into the millennium by the number runner to see how long John and I would remain solvent.

"Right here," said the accountant, a serious man in his thirties, tapping a manicured fingernail on a computer printout line representing our state of affairs in the year 2030. He had been talking us through a sheaf of charts that took us into our dotage. Things had been going fairly well until he got to the box where I was 85 and John was 78. "Right here, according to my best calculations, is where the money runs out."

"Runs out?" I asked, stunned. "You mean, like, it's gone? Zip? Nothing in the ATM?"

"Not much."

"Are we dead?"

"Yes," my husband answered. "We blew what was left in 2029 and then drank the Kool-Aid."

Our investment manager hadn't made so much as a squeak about the money running out. He was a sunny, puckish man who enjoyed giving people good news. "You're fine," he said after he ran the numbers. "You can retire and do anything you want." Maybe he hadn't run the numbers the same way. Or maybe he crunched them. Crunching was probably the way to make numbers behave. Grab the little devils by their throats, throw them into the blender, and punch the "chop" button. I wanted to call the puckish adviser, ask him about his blender, and have him talk sense to the accountant.

But I didn't because I knew both men were right. That is the hell of personal finance. Beyond the basic axioms of *Everyone should have savings, Diversity is a good thing in investments,* and *Restrain yourself from plunking it all on a Beemer or the long shot in the Kentucky Derby,* money is a matter of opinion. Go to 10 different financial experts and sort through 10 different answers, all of them possible. And maybe one or two might suggest buying the Beemer or placing the bet.

This is Wizard of Oz country. Not that it's populated by phonies. It's just that the accuracy of the prognostications depends as much on the variables of the coming economic winds as on the courage, heart, brain, and risk tolerance of the individual seeking advice.

But people want to believe there's an oracle out there with The Answer. That's why the advice industry has thrived, telling people what they can take to the bank and how they can retire happy, retire rich, retire happy *and* rich, retire financially free (whatever that means), or retire generally smarter than the rest of the folks who are consulting their gurus. The oracles run seminars, write newsletters, come out with "idiot" guides, and all those eight-step, 10-step, or 12-step plans for success. And they have multiplied as Baby Boomers have moved into retirement.

They fill whole sections in bookstores and the titles are breathless — *Create Your Retirement: 55 Ways to Empower the Rest of Your Life* by Barbara M. Walker, or *Prime Time: How Baby Boomers Will Revolutionize Retirement and Transform America*, by Marc Freedman.

The titles are smug — *Retiring Right* by Lawrence J. Kaplan. They're dry — *The Evolution of Retirement*, by Dora L. Costa. They're bizarre — *Planning Your Rare Coin Retirement* by David Ganz. And they're scary — *Don't Die Broke* by Margaret Malaspina. I bet she wrote it after talking to her accountant.

"Remember, these are conservative estimates," our accountant explained, trying to get our minds off the empty ATM machine. He smiled the way doctors do when they want to calm the patient who has just received bad news. "I low-balled earnings and high-balled expenses. You're doing okay. Really. Compared to some people who come in here, you're in good, solid, middle-of-the-road shape. Not great, but good."

The look on my face must have told him I wanted him to go back to Pamplona and open a different gate. A couple days later, he sent an e-mail saying he had good news. He'd tweaked the numbers and the money wouldn't run out until 2034.

But how real was this number? And how depressed would I get focusing on it?

Not as depressed as I would get talking to the financial planner, who called one day on the recommendation of a friend who had used his services. The planner said he'd like to run the numbers and sit down with John and me to discuss options. Making conversation, he said, ever so casually, "Figure you'll live another 30 years. You'll want to have a portfolio that reflects that." There it was, dropped into the sentence as though it were the weather report — 30 years left. And if he was right, that meant I'd be retired two years less than the number of years I'd worked, which seemed out of balance somehow. I didn't want the office to win.

Of course, 30 was a number the planner had plucked from life-expectancy statistics and insurance actuarial tables. It had nothing to do with me personally, and yet it felt intensely personal hearing a stranger on the phone calculate the time left on my clock.

It was a nice round number, as numbers go, a biggish digit that friends who had died way too young would have cheered had they heard it from their doctors. They would have cheered 15, 10, or even five. So I felt ungrateful wishing he hadn't mentioned it. I was like the pessimist frowning at a half-empty glass of water, which would have been half full had I been an optimist.

Another 30 years. That meant the planner figured my life at age 60 was two-thirds gone. Maybe this should have been obvious, but I hadn't looked at it that way. Numbers had been like a foreign language since grade school, when I wrote them backwards, couldn't get the fundamentals of making change, and had trouble counting it in Monopoly games. I learned to avoid numbers and focus on words, which were a lot friendlier and could be spun into fantasy.

But the money oracles don't do fantasy.

"Are you healthy?" the accountant asked, and I nodded. "Then don't start taking Social Security until age 66." He said that if I wasn't healthy and thought I might check out before age 78, I should start taking Social Security at age 62.

The investment adviser had said just the opposite. Healthy or not, waiting was a bad idea. "Always take the money when you can," he said, noting that the government Social Security fund might be gone by the time I reached 66, and that would mean missing out on five years of checks, which was worse than waiting for more money later.

Unless it wasn't. Unless waiting was the right answer. But there was no right answer, right? Just advice and gut feelings. Just attitude. Just the spinning roulette wheel in the big casino of life, and time. Nobody knew who was going to outlive their money or whose money would be left on the table.

Could I live with that? Yes and no. I wanted to. It was probably the only way to live.

CHAPTER 4

Way Off the Clock

"I don't know how I had time to work."

Retired people love to say this, and I always want to tell them how they did it. They had time to work because they got the hell out of the house in the morning. They got into the car, into the office, and into the desk chair, and they got things done, more or less. At least they looked as though they were getting things done. They had a boss with a schedule who worked for a company with a schedule and the company was a fairly regular contributor to the gross domestic product. So there were expectations, and the expectations were met.

There were clocks in this company, and everyone knew what time it was and what was supposed to get done before lunch. Even if all that got done before lunch was an e-mail explaining why the work wouldn't be done until after lunch, it was considered a reasonable accomplishment for the morning. Information had been exchanged. People had nodded. Maybe a meeting had been scheduled.

In an office, even a wasted day is still a payday. People feel tired at the end of it. They come home and say, "Whew!" They take off their shoes and put on comfortable clothes, convinced they have earned those comfortable clothes because, by God, they worked. They have, as the phrase goes, "managed their time" for eight hours or longer and are now "off the clock."

But the truth is they didn't manage time at all. Time managed them the whole day and most likely continued to manage them into the evening as they answered e-mails, took cell-phone calls, and went through the briefcase full of reading. They did this until time dictated sleep and the setting of the alarm. The next morning, time managed the minutes allowed for pounding the snooze button and for getting to the gym or taking the morning walk, which may have been no more than a couple of steps into the driveway to retrieve the newspaper because time had been wasted hitting the snooze button too often.

Time managed the reading of that newspaper and how much print could be absorbed below the headlines. It managed the sprint into the shower and whether that shower was leisurely or perfunctory. It governed the gulping of the second cup of coffee and the possibility of a third purchased on the road to the expressway. It controlled the flow of sweat leaking into the armpits if the expressway was once again an oxymoron with a tractor trailer rig jackknifed north of Boston and traffic stalled back into Rhode Island.

People who think they manage time and call themselves efficiency experts usually have a staff to carry the load. Or they practice their art by writing books and giving seminars on organizational skills that most people don't have time to absorb because they live in the White Rabbit, working stiff, real world where there is barely a minute to say "hello/good-bye" while racing for the meeting room, the sales call, or the plane. And that's what people love, and hate, about their jobs. They're busy, too busy, and busy people are important.

As a newspaper reporter, I was chained to time. The adrenaline rush of journalism was beating the clock while trying not to choke, while writing too fast to think too much, pounding on a laptop in a hotel room with an editor on the phone demanding copy for an early first edition: "Send what you got!"

Send. Now. We want. They want. Gotta have it. Go get it.

Other businesses are just as intense, sometimes more so, when millions of dollars are riding on the speed of the assembly line, the ability of the marketing team to meet third-quarter projections, or the shipping department's agility in filling holiday orders that are already 10 days late.

Tick, tick, tick. Tock, tock, tock. See Dick run. See Jane fly. Grab a pizza and eat it in the car. Get dressed while packing the school lunches. Look down while dashing in from the office parking lot to discover that one shoe is black and the other is brown. And the voice of sanity whispers: *Someday you're gonna live like a normal person. Someday you're gonna get off this flippin' treadmill and stop. Do you hear me? STOP!*

And one day you do. And so does time. And it's glorious and like no place you've been since summer vacation back in grade school. It feels a little like the silence in the house after the electricity goes off in a summer-night storm. All the gizmos stop humming, and a velvety blackness opens the pupils wide to a world with softer shapes.

It is a lovely place to be after the noise and frustration and exhaustion of a career. It is an oasis. But in the quiet of days unclaimed and unformed like rich clay about to be thrown against a potter's wheel, a realization presses slowly into the consciousness with unexpected weight: *The moment has come for me to manage time. Really manage time. Acres of it for years, solo. No 9:00 A.M. start. No 10:00 A.M. meeting. No closing bell. No deadline. Nothing but the uncharted day and limitless possibility.*

And so you and time stand in the middle of the living room staring at each other after all those sweaty years and try to redefine your relationship. Maybe you swagger a little. Why not? You earned this. You swagger on over to the old boss and say "Na-na-na-NA-NA, Time! Can't touch me now because you know what? I'm drivin' the bus and it's your turn to follow my schedule. And I got plans, sweetheart. I got lists. I got books to write, books to read, classes to take, important things to do. We are going places."

Time just smiles, shrugs, and folds without an argument. Maybe it stretches out on the couch for awhile and closes its eyes. Then it vanishes, drifting off to wherever it goes in the houses of retired people.

Away is where it goes. It evaporates into the ether, weasels out through a crack in the universe, and plops into a black hole while you're messing with string in the kitchen drawer and not writing a novel or joining the Peace Corps or planning a trip to the Orient or doing much of anything worth talking about.

Why is there so much string in kitchen drawers, and why does it attach itself to the Scotch tape and fuzzy half-melted LifeSavers? How can a morning go by while you're untangling string from LifeSavers and looking for a box to hold stray rubber bands, driving to the office-supply store to buy one of those organizer things with little compartments, looking at a couple aisles full of them, and coming home to decide not to put the one purchased — which may go back — on the kitchen counter, but on the desk, which is loaded with stuff that has to get organized to make room for the organizer?

When I worked, I had everything filed and labeled and I didn't do tangents. I was so riveted I'd jump if somebody walked into the office. No way could I go out to lunch. No way could I answer the phone. Door shut, eyes focused on the computer screen, shoulders hunched, I did the job word by word, tick by tock, straight on, without experiencing any sudden urges to haul out a vacuum cleaner.

At home I discovered dust. Sitting on the toilet one morning, I looked up and there it was. Who had time to do that with a full-time job? Who had time to finish the constitutional, get a stepladder out of the closet, and stand up there with a vacuum cleaner hose slung over one shoulder while working the long, flat upholstery cushion tool into the slats of the ceiling vent to suck out gray gunk at 9:00 in the morning?

How long had the gunk been up there? Where did it come from? How could it cling to the edges of the vent in little rounded clumps and not drop to the floor? Did I want to know? Would somebody at Harvard or MIT like to do experiments on it and find out?

Pondering these and other great questions, I discovered mold. It started in the corner of the bathroom ceiling where the paint was flaking — another discovery — and was making its way out past the vent toward the door in a trail of small brown spots.

I got down off the stepladder, shoved the vacuum cleaner into the hall, and poured bleach into a bucket. I put on rubber gloves, soaked a sponge in the bleach, balanced once again on the ladder, and scrubbed at the brown spots. The sponge crumbled against the rough surface of the ceiling and sent little pink fragments onto the floor. So I got down, dragged the vacuum cleaner back into the bathroom, and swept up the sponge droppings, some of which had shot into the linen closet. I went after them.

In the linen closet, I discovered old towels. They had to go, along with old detergents, dried shoe polish, and cough medicine that expired in 2002. When did we use ACE bandages? Was the heating pad the one that charred skin or was this the replacement? Three hair dryers? Get real.

And more dust. Bigger dust, sprawling colonies of dust that were probably the breeding ground for the stuff in the vent. The scale on the floor under the bottom shelf of the linen closet was so thick with it that the numbers were unreadable. The jug of distilled water seemed to be putting down roots, and the dust cloths jammed up against the back wall looked as though they were about to surrender.

I vacuumed. I sorted. I tossed. I looked at the clock. Noon. Was it possible to spend half a day in the bathroom? There was still mold on the ceiling, and I had not begun to shop for bananas.

Buying bananas, buying anything, became a kind of Zen meditation on the nuances of texture and the communal experience of commerce. Before retiring, I had watched people shop that way and wanted to ram them with my cart. *Get ON with it, already. It's a banana, not a piece of the Holy Grail.* I'd blitz through the store with the last spurt of post-work energy, intent on getting out the door and home with something, anything, edible. The store was full of people like me at 6:30 or 7:00 at night, people with pinched, tired office faces, people clutching frozen pizzas and not daring to read the ingredients, people figuring that at least one corner of hell would have to be a super-market where there was no logical arrangement to the merchandise on the shelves and no way to turn down the Muzak grinding Beatles songs into sawdust.

Shopping by day during the week was a slow-motion video, a stroll through Grocery Land, where people often acted as though they were visiting for the first time. They studied product boxes, compared listings of ingredients with those on other boxes, discussed the pending decision with spouses, worked with calculators, sorted through coupons, read articles in the magazine aisles, and hummed a tune that may, or may not, have been the one coming over the loudspeaker.

And I hummed along with them. I'd chat, too, and say, "Remember that song? It came out when I was in high school."

I shopped for figs. Never bought a fig in my life when I worked. Now I was going to three stores, hunting them down for a meat loaf sauce. And I went into two stores looking for a meat loaf pan. Had the ruler with me in the purse to measure the dimensions and make sure it was 9 by 5 by 3 inches like the recipe said.

I drove to a couple of towns looking for something called "fenugreek seed," but didn't find it, and I'm still not sure what it is. I bought fennel, too, and put it on fish. Fennel! I used to think it was weird celery.

And I picked through mountains of bananas, looking for the small ones without bruises, taking care to feel for invisible soft spots, selecting three or four fine specimens in varying colors, deep green to almost-ripe yellow so that they wouldn't all turn black at once.

I could go into the grocery store, take side trips to the

drugstore and the hardware store, and blow an afternoon. I could come home and blow another couple hours answering e-mail, or going through adult-education catalogues, weighing the choices: tai chi or yoga? Poetry workshop or short-story writing? Was there time for both? What was happening to time?

Studying the crowded squares of the calendar, mentally moving things around on pages already full of cross-outs and arrows, I saw a note to myself: "Get Dante's *Inferno*." The book group was meeting to discuss *The Dante Club* by Matthew Pearl, and I wanted *Inferno* on tape to hear it read out loud the way a character in Pearl's book hears it. I drove to the library, found the tape, and then spent the rest of the day in the Middle Ages.

Was life getting a little fragmented? Was I wasting time or just getting comfortable with having a lot of it? Was retirement not so much about taking control as it was about learning to love a tangent? Was I asking the right questions?

There was a snort from somewhere in the black hole beyond the crack in the universe where time, swinging gently in a hammock, said, "You're drivin' the bus, Sweetheart. You are drivin' the bus."

CHAPTER 5

Carcass Maintenance

I drew the line at seeing a physiatrist. I'd never heard of physiatry, and it rhymed with "psychiatry," which would be the next stop if I didn't get a grip and just live with the sciatica, or whatever was causing the tight leg muscle.

Was that the right decision? Who knows? The health and fitness thing, like the rest of retirement, can absorb as much time as a person wishes to pour into it. The challenge is to find the balance between being sensibly "pro-active," as they say in the medical articles, and turning into a nut.

Conversations with friends teetered on that fulcrum, and when we reached the tipping point in the wrong direction, we self-corrected with jokes.

"You'll never guess what I'm taking for the arthritis — cod-liver oil! Ha, ha, ha. I sound like my grandmother."

"Ha, ha, ha. Where can I get it?"

We've been to college, had careers, and now are writing poetry, fiction, and plays, going to museums, taking courses, teaching courses, and growing — oh we talk a lot about growth and the great wide canvas of the 60-plus years, and it is all true. But there is also that stiffness. And there are those stretches that have to be done every morning, *have* to be done. No more voluntary whimsical limbering up to keep the fine tone and cat-like grace. Just hard-core, basic "carcass maintenance," as my friend Liz calls it. She lives in San Francisco, where people are in touch with their bodies and do tai chi in the park at dawn. That sounds exotic, but it's work and she will tell you that. Rowing in the bay is work. Swimming is work, more work than it used to be. The movement is mandatory if one wants to keep moving.

The calcium and vitamin D are mandatory. Being "an informed consumer," the watchwords of the Baby Boomer generation, is mandatory. Being a careful researcher of the Web, knowing what questions to ask, and being a partner in one's care are all mandatory and locked into the presumption that if one does all that, one will not get old, at least not the way Grandma did.

How much easier life was when doctors were gods. They'd grunt, look austere sitting under their medical degrees in their white jackets, and write a prescription. Patients did what they were told. "The doctor said," was all anybody needed to know.

Now there's a lot more smiling, maybe because there are a lot more lawsuits. The doctor shares brochures and free samples. The doctor recommends. The doctor says, "You might want to consider seeing a physiatrist."

That's a specialist who diagnoses and treats musculoskeletal pain, which is what I thought a physical therapist did. It *is* what a physical therapist does, but a physiatrist does more of it.

Did I want more of it?

The primary care physician had recommended the physical therapist, who, after eight weeks of workouts, said, "I think the problem could be the bunion on your left foot," and recommended a podiatrist. The podiatrist said, "It doesn't look like a bottom-up problem to me," and held out a piece of paper with the physiatrist's name on it.

Calling a new specialist would mean more medical appointments filling the squares of the calendar, maybe more pills on the kitchen counter, and more things to do to keep fit, or to give me fits in the morning, which already involved a 40-minute health regimen. I did three neck exercises, shoulder rolls, and back stretches while sitting in a chair. I did waist swings and toe touches while standing up, followed by a workout with a thick, black Thera-Band, one end in each fist for more neck and arm strengthening. I did doorjamb and wall-leaning exercises and a floor routine for the lower back and legs that included lifts and push-ups and finished with yoga.

Each movement had been recommended by a body-part expert with the promise that it would take "just a few minutes a day," and individually, each one did. But all together they were a gym class. Throw in the protocols for my aging cats — preparation of special kidney diet food, high-blood-pressure and thyroid medications, massaging of their arthritic backs, and, for a while, salve on a sore paw and Prozac gel in an ear — and I could blow over an hour on carcass care before getting mine out the door for a walk.

No way could I have done that with a full-time job. The best I did then was a shorter walk and no stretching before hunching over the newspapers to look for editorial ideas. At the office, I hunched over the computer keyboard for most of the day, give or take bathroom and coffee breaks. Lunch was a hunch at the desk while typing. There was a yoga class in the building, but who had time? Somewhere around 6:00 at night, I'd get in the car, hunch over the steering wheel, and inch home in the rush-hour traffic.

Retirement meant the freedom to stop doing that and move around, to pay attention to the body I'd ignored — abused was more like it. It wasn't hypochondria that drove me into the medical garage for diagnostics and tune-ups, but a sense of finally being able to get at the physical problems the way one gets at the funny noise in the transmission or the loose connection in the wiring. The feeling was, "Okay, let's fix the damn thing and move on."

But one diagnostic test can lead to another. One doctor can lead to another. One item in a health product catalogue can lead to another, especially in a foot-care catalogue, and especially if the feet were hurting when I read it. The feet did not hurt all the time. Constant pain might have been easier to diagnose and fix. Sporadic, quirky pain took one on a quest through hammertoe straighteners, toe separators, callous pads, bunion protectors, corn removers, heel cups, neuroma cushions, and arch supports, all tried a couple of times and then tossed into a shoe box in the closet.

"Most of that stuff doesn't work," the podiatrist had said as he handed me some metatarsal pads along with the physiatrist's name. He was right. His pads didn't work either. No, I take that back. They kind of worked sometimes on the pain between the toes — not to be confused with the tight leg muscle that brought me to his office in the first place. But, like all the foot remedies jammed in the shoe box, the pads seemed to be an improvement for a short time before they began to feel strange. How soon the items in the collection began to feel strange, and a lot like pain, varied and bore no relation to logic. One day they were okay; the next day they weren't. I tried custom orthotics, too, but after a honeymoon that seemed to be turning into a stable marriage, they went south and hurt as much as the leather arch supports from the drugstore.

New shoes were just as erratic, behaving themselves in the store or on the living-room rug when the price sticker was still on their soles, but turning vicious and a half size too small as soon as they were taken out for a walk, an evening event, or anywhere dirt and scuff marks rendered them nonreturnable.

There are retired people who can wear high heels. I have seen them, dancing. But as the years have passed, I have sunk lower into the floor and dared to wear SAS sandals as dress shoes — to the Boston Symphony. I went to a ballroom-dance event in them too, which looked bizarre, but felt so much better than anything that would have looked good.

If aging brings on a second childhood, then I am Goldilocks, stumbling through a marketplace where the choices are too big, too small, too tight, too loose, too long, too short, too dowdy, or too young. Finding what is "just right" can take days, though it used to take hours. And in a mattress store it can take years.

John and I are sleeping on our third bed in seven years. It is a deluxe model with "breathable" cashmere innards, layers of "memory foam and latex," and an "advanced coil system." It replaced the bed that was too soft, which replaced the one that was too hard, which replaced the one that was just about right for 14 years. The 14-year wonder had been a cheapo, discount model from a warehouse store. We purchased it as newlyweds, gave it a cursory lie-down in the showroom, and said "Yeah, fine, we'll take it." And it was fine, and we were 24 years younger, and lots of things were working better than they do now, and we didn't care about advanced coils.

Our second mattress came from a beautiful-bed store where "sleep technicians" wore white smocks like a medical team and the overhead lights dimmed when people stretched out on the beds. A man with a clipboard followed us around, answering questions about springs, pillow tops, and what "sleep systems" worked best with what body types. He asked about burgeoning back problems and bad necks, and directed us to "cushioning." He said we needed "give," and looked doubtful when we chose "firm" because that's what we thought was good for the spine.

The man in white with the clipboard was right, but it took us three years to admit it. We kept thinking we were "getting used to it," "breaking it in." Our shoulders and arms went numb in the night, and rolling over would have gone easier with a grappling hook. But, by God, we bought our bed and we were going to lie in it. I should have known what we were dealing with when the literature that came with the bed's limited warranty included this sentence: "Adjusting to a new mattress is like adjusting to a new pair of shoes."

We had purchased the $1,500 lumbar equivalent of a bad pair of loafers. The 60-day trial period was long over, and the thing had us right by the sacrum. So we ate our pride, and money, went back to the beautiful-bed store, promised never to doubt the people in white again, and threw ourselves on the softest mattress in the showroom. Ahhhhh. Lights out.

But a year later, the thing started to crater.

"Maybe it just feels like you're sinking into a pit because the last mattress felt like Plymouth Rock," I suggested.

"It feels like I'm sinking into a pit because I'm sinking into a pit," John growled.

The months passed, and the pit grew bigger and deeper. Two years in, there was one growing on my side of the mattress.

"This is not happening," I whispered into the darkness.

"Yeah, it is," John said, his voice slightly muffled by natural fibers.

"Let's try to work with it," I insisted, stuffing pillows under the small of my back. We rotated the mattress every couple of weeks. We tried flipping it, even though it supposedly never needed flipping. Then we flipped it back.

The bed had a lifetime guarantee for replacement, but I figured the problem was us and didn't want to complain *again*.

"Complain," John said.

After sending two inspectors out to the house to study our pits, the beautiful-bed store made good on its guarantee. We could exchange The Sinker for anything in the showroom. Anything. That was great news, but intimidating as hell because the store allowed just one exchange. Blow this free pick and we could be going back to the accountant.

We did research. We visited bed stores, read consumer critiques on Web sites, talked to friends and asked to stretch out on their beds. We discussed the relative merits of platforms, foam, water, and feathers. We took notes in hotels, crawled around on the floor looking for labels, and inquired at the desk about the age of the bed in our room. We studied the ads: "You Spend

One-Third of Your Life in Bed"; "How Much Is Great Sleep Worth?"; "Better Sleep, Better Health, Better Bed." Were we ready to choose yet again? The carcass was waiting.

"Maybe we should go back to the discount warehouse and buy another cheapie," John said.

But we'd become far too sophisticated — or maybe far too gullible in believing something pretty close to perfection is possible. We went back to the beautiful-bed store with the exchange papers and, after our longest deliberation yet, which included having a reading done on a machine that measured our "pressure points," we chose a mattress so big and so heavy it took three guys to haul it into the house with several rest stops. This mattress cannot be flipped or rotated. Ever. It can hardly be shoved an inch this way or that. And it's so high that I climb in at night with a little hop. The cats can't make it without a footstool.

The bed is way better than the last two, but it's not perfect. There are body indentations. Will they grow? There are mornings when everything aches. There are times when I think I hate it and other times when it seems okay. But if it goes south, I sure can't toss it in the shoe box in the closet.

Life just might have been more relaxed when buying a bed was as uncomplicated as a doctor visit. The plethora of choices and depth of detail in everything we do and are supposed to know could be keeping us awake at night.

Is that healthy? Yes, no, and maybe. I have a physiatrist's name if anybody would like a second opinion.

↦ CHAPTER 6 ↤

In the Zone

Learning how not to have a 9-to-5 job anymore is a little like learning how to play tennis, only slower. Some days, the retirement game is nowhere, the feet don't move, the follow-through is lousy, and the eye loses the ball. Other days, magic happens. Ball, body, and psyche are in The Zone in stunning synch. The magic comes in an instant and can vanish just as quickly, but before it goes, it whispers: *You are exactly where you should be.*

I have been in The Zone in midmorning phone conversations with friends, no longer rushed. I have been there at lunches when the talk continues into late afternoon. I have been there in gas station lines and at red lights when the wait no longer feels like an insult but a nice little pause. I have been there on a weekday bird walk with a guide who could identify everything he heard and who directed all eyes way up to a scarlet tanager preening in the sun.

And I have been there on a warm December day waiting for a Green Line car in Coolidge Corner after a funeral. It was

2006, and Muriel Cohen had died at age 86. She had covered education at the *Boston Globe* and at the *Boston Herald* before that, although "covered" is too bland a word. She lived the beat and rarely got beat. She was the blunt, unrelenting newsroom mother to many of us, taking young reporters under her iron wing, pushing us to do better, and telling us to shape up if the reporting got sloppy, if we wimped out on asking for a raise, or if the wardrobe needed oxygen.

"Don't sit there like a lump," she said, looming over my desk with a group of women in tow. It was spring, 1978, and I'd just found out I'd been passed over for a Nieman Fellowship to Harvard. "We're taking you out to lunch to celebrate."

"Celebrate? I lost."

"I know you lost," she snapped, ever impatient with time wasted on the obvious. "This is a loser's lunch. Very exclusive. We're celebrating you."

Twenty-eight years later, I could hear her voice in the funeral chapel. I hadn't seen her much since she'd retired. She had called over the years with invitations to birthday parties and other gatherings she organized for her newsroom daughters, but my deadlines were tighter than they had been in the 1970s, and, more to the point, I was tighter.

"I can't," I'd tell her, hearing the exasperated sigh on the other end of the line.

"Yes you can."

She was right, but I'd lost touch with people while doing my job in the communications business. Had I been working when she died, I might not have gone to the funeral. I certainly would not have lingered afterward to hug former colleagues or to walk over to a Starbucks for a long talk with a pal who had flown up from Washington for the gathering. We shared what felt like a communion cup as we drank dark roast at a small table and reminisced, and I could hear Muriel shout, "Finally, already, she gets it!"

Had I been working, I would have raced back to the office, nervous about what needed to be done rather than experiencing what needed to be absorbed. I would not have walked slowly up Harvard Street to Beacon Street feeling the blessing of the unseasonably mild weather or sat on a bench in the sun, not caring if the trolley was late. When it pulled up, crowded and noisy, I remained on the bench and waited for the next train. It came soon enough without me once scowling at my wristwatch.

You are exactly where you should be. The words kept time with the trolley car motion as it rumbled to Park Street. What a luxury to be able to hear it, to have a grip on the small things that are huge, the things that get buried like pyramids under the daily sandstorms of schedules and demands.

The Zone is fusion with the present, being there, being alive, connecting. I'm in it with my 91-year-old friend, Jean, who buys books by the shopping bag and maintains a broad view of the world from her apartment looking out on the woods and the river. I have known her for 42 years but have treasured time now to know her better.

I had time to get to know Eloise, a genuine old-fashioned Southern lady who moved north at age 90. She was the mother of a friend and lived in a lovely assisted-living home in Cohasset. She would tell me about growing up in North Carolina, and I would tell her about growing up in Ohio. We looked at old photos, told jokes, and exchanged books. One afternoon we opened her Southern Baptist hymnal and sang — off-key but loud.

She died in 2009 at age 92. I miss visiting her every Tuesday at 4:00 — deadline hour in my old life. I don't miss the deadlines.

If I hadn't retired, I would not have joined a book club, something I'd wanted to join for 20 years. Every month, the circle of six to a dozen women gathers — first at the local Barnes & Noble, now around a table in a flower shop belonging to one of the women. They are nurses, retirees, homemakers, teachers, and businesspeople. They are people I would not have met in a job that left me little energy for reading more than a couple of books a year. The year I retired, I read 15:

Hotel Du Lac, Anita Brookner
Girls, Frederick Busch
Founding Brothers, Joseph Ellis
His Excellency: George Washington, Joseph Ellis
American Sphinx : The Character of Thomas Jefferson,
  Joseph Ellis
Fahrenheit 451, Ray Bradbury
Case Histories, Kate Atkinson
The Dogs of Babel, Carolyn Parkhurst
Snow Flower and the Secret Fan, Lisa See
The Satanic Verses, Salman Rushdie
The Dancing Girls of Lahore, Louise Brown
The Catcher in the Rye, J. D. Salinger
Brave New World, Aldous Huxley
Many Lives, Many Masters, Brian L. Weiss
Tuesdays with Morrie, Mitch Albom

I am proud of that list, but it's puny compared to the 40-plus volumes some of the other women read annually as members of several clubs and as people who just naturally pick up books the way magnets pick up metal. They are people who think about American culture, who can talk politics as intelligently as they can discuss the possibilities of reincarnation. They laugh loudly at themselves but take the written word seriously, and they worry that many young people don't. They are passionate and plugged in, but old-school, solid, grounded in knowing exactly who they are.

I look around the circle as nine o'clock approaches, feeling energized instead of exhausted, holding the clutch of books I inevitably buy or borrow, and am the kid I used to be on the porch in the summer, reading away the days.

I'm a kid in the pool, too, doing water aerobics, something that a lot of athletes consider a joke. The athletes are wrong. We come together, six, eight, 10, or 15 strong at 8:00 A.M. We jump and splash to rock music and rediscover a piece of childhood in the noise and buoyancy. We're in day camp again with the coolest counselor, Amy, who is also the toughest and makes everyone sweat, telling us to whirl the foam weights over our heads, circle them out to the side, or push them back and forth under water. "And press and press and press," she shouts. "Don't die out on me!"

"The nine o'clock class couldn't take this," we say, standing taller, sucking in stomachs, confident that the 50- and 60-plus bulges are turning into something good, and they are, even with a few sags. We push our individual envelopes, not caring how sleek and slick the bodies are in the weight room, where they think we're old people.

We don't know each other's last names, but we are family and worry if someone doesn't show for a week. We ask about

43

each other's backs and knees. We talk recipes and grandchildren. We gather around Kate when she comes back in the fall after the death of her husband. We hug Nancy as she leaves on what will be a last vacation for her dying husband. Nancy — tiny, athletic, and beautiful — presses her weights up and down in the splashing line, looks straight ahead with a determined smile, and gives us our *carpe diem:* "One day you're healthy, and then you're not. That's how life goes. Don't take anything for granted."

Put it on a sampler. Hang it on the wall. Remember the lessons of The Zone.

And when I forget, when the eyes aren't focused on the ball and magic is buried in the laundry hamper, when I am bound by insecurities, confusion, aches, and a fear of drifting, I read the poetry of Danna Faulds. Her work was introduced to me in a yoga class led by Elizabeth, an instructor who survived breast cancer and who eased her panic about that disease through the postures of an ancient practice.

In "It Doesn't Always Smell Like Roses,"* Faulds writes:

*This body is not flowing
with liquid energy, no,
and this mind is not
awash with peace. I
fight myself in every
posture, muscles shriek,
fear freezes bone and a
sure sense of failure grows.*

*This too is practice,
this ground where grief*

gains the upper hand,
and anger casts dark
shadows. This, the flip
side of delight is as much
the point as any pleasure —
this is breathing into life.

In "Full Moon,"* she writes:

The moon leaned her full,
round face so close to mine
that her mountains touched
the furrows of my brow.

"I have a secret," she said
with a wink. I waited.
"You're not dead until you're
dead," she said. I was a bit
incredulous.

"You're not impressed?" the
moon asked, looking just a
bit perplexed. "Well, let me
put it this way then.

"You've got every single day that
you're alive to really live. Isn't
that due cause for celebration?"
Her enthusiasm was infectious.

The moon bent low, just missing
a collision with a flying wedge of
geese. "So, what are you doing
this evening?" she asked. "I'm

being me," I said. "Oh, that's
the best!" the moon replied, and
smiling widely, resumed
her place in the starlit sky.

*Poems reprinted with permission from Danna Faulds.
"It Doesn't Always Smell Like Roses" from her book *Go In and In*; "Full Moon"
from her book *One Soul*

CHAPTER 7

Alice

Alice was my 86-year-old mother-in-law. Her last year of life was my first year of retirement, and that made us a kind of alpha-omega duo. Maybe omega and pre-omega is a better description. Either way, we were both groping.

As she lost her mind to dementia and her body to cancer in a nearby assisted-living facility, she took me on an intimate daily tour of frail old age — the place that is not for sissies, the place much of American culture chooses to erase from the consciousness because it's not about trim gray-haired people playing tennis and golf in an active adult retirement community. It's about dying. And Alice taught me that it's also very much about living.

I'd never had the tour before, not even with my parents. They died relatively young, way too fast, and determinedly independent. I was a visitor then, flying down to Orlando from Washington or Boston, taking time off from the newspaper job to be with them for one or two weeks. I didn't quite get what was happening and maybe didn't want to get it. Until their last days, they made their medical decisions and were my parents as they had always been.

My dad was making jokes with the nurses and doing crossword puzzles as he lay in the hospital in the final stages of lung cancer at age 69. His passing on a February morning in 1983 was a jolt, a rap I thought he still might beat. My mother, who died of respiratory failure 12 years later at age 76, had insisted she was fine, gasping for breath as the EMTs carried her out of her house on a stretcher. She and my dad didn't want hand-holding. They didn't want caregivers (least of all if their kids were giving the care), and they had probably never heard the word, which is so common today. They seemed to run off life's stage in the middle of their big scenes, lines unspoken, my dad going less than a year after being diagnosed, and my mother doggedly refusing to be diagnosed. After they were gone, I felt there was still so much to say.

Alice faded slowly, incrementally yet inexorably, leaving little unsaid. She shuffled away, slept away, drifted away over years to the place the Irish call "with the fairies," and Alzheimer's families call "the long good-bye." She wanted care, demanded it, and, at her best, was grateful for every piece of folded laundry, cup of Starbucks coffee, box of candy, ride to the shore for ice cream, and trip to the doctor. She would beg John and me to stay longer, no matter how long we had been with her. "You can sleep here," she'd say, not comprehending that our house was only a 10-minute drive across town. "I'll make up a bed on the couch. Don't go. Sit and talk to me."

She was a child, shrunken and small. She clung to us not only for immediate company but because we were her memory. We held her life in our undamaged minds like a fine leather scrapbook that we could open at any time. When she was with us, or with her niece, Mary, or nephew, Jerry, who would visit from Canada, she felt safe.

"My memory's shot to hell," she'd say in a moment of disgusted clarity as she grasped for a name, a place, or a common noun, which became "the whatchamacallit." We weren't sure what was worse — grim self-awareness or the days when her voice became dreamy and she'd tell us her mother was coming to take her home.

I'd known Alice for 20 years. We met in 1986, the year John and I were married. He introduced us in his Washington apartment and cooked us dinner. As we raised our wine glasses for a toast, mine slipped from a nervous hand and shattered on the floor next to her foot. "Oh, Mrs. Stobierski, I'm so sorry," I said, reaching down to clean up.

"It's 'Alice,'" she said. "And you missed me. So you'll have to try that again."

She took me shopping that weekend in Washington and bought me Oscar de la Renta perfume. I bought her a hat. We shopped together into her last year, although she had to go in a wheelchair then and no longer had the stamina to make an afternoon of it. And when she got home, she didn't recognize what was in the bags.

But she'd still say, "Susan, let me buy you something." She was still the woman who wanted to go out to lunch, insisting, "My treat. And we're getting dessert." She was still the woman who easily accepted my not being Catholic, even though she was devout. "I love you so much," she'd say often, even on days when we'd argued.

On good days, she could still tell her stories. There was the time she and John's father mistakenly walked into a bowling-league dinner instead of a wedding reception at a country club holding several events simultaneously. "We kept eating hors d'oeuvres and looking around for somebody we knew," Alice would say. "They were all down the hall."

She once left her suitcase behind in the driveway as she headed for the airport to catch a flight to Canada. "I arrived with a pair of earrings and a bottle of Scotch," she'd say with a sweep of her hand.

It was my job to remember that, and to tell her the stories when she had forgotten them. "I did that?" she'd say, surprised, delighted. When she was angry or depressed, refusing to take medicine or to take a shower or to put on clean clothes, it was my job to remember the funny, magnanimous lady who once dressed with flair, knew what to do with her drawer full of terrific scarves, and loved a party. When she couldn't dial the phone anymore and confused it with the TV channel clicker, it was my job to remember the smart lady who had been the well-liked manager in the Connecticut social services department. It was my job to remember the lady who would have been appalled at seeing herself slumped in a chair two decades later, unaware of food stains on her blouse.

"How about wearing one of your new outfits," I'd say, pulling a pair of slacks and matching top out of the closet.

"I'm too tired. Don't make me change."

I'd try to cajole her with a bottle of cologne, telling her we'd spritz it behind each ear after she took a sponge bath and put on fresh clothes. I'd assure her that a sponge bath was way easier than a shower, which she had come to detest because she was afraid of the flying water and couldn't remember how the knob worked.

On good days, Alice would sigh and say, "Yes, Mother. Anything you say, Mother. I do what I'm told." On bad days, she'd tell me to shut up and stop ordering her around. She'd grab her cane and head for the door. On *really* bad days, she'd tell me she could walk just fine without a cane and would leave it leaning against her chair.

Slowly, during that last year, I learned I had to let her go. Not always, but more than I wanted to. The challenge was figuring out which times. That's a parent's biggest challenge too, I think, although I don't have children. Maybe learning when to let go is the biggest challenge for anybody who loves another person. When do you butt out and stop trying to help? When do you let someone risk a fall?

I became a juggler of risks. Should we go into the restaurant where the floors might be slippery and a kid might accidentally knock her off balance? Should we go to the beach where the ground is uneven?

I became a juggler of time — how much for her, how much for me? That also made me a juggler of guilt when I took more for me and decided her message on the answering machine wasn't urgent. I became a juggler of moods, learning when to keep quiet and listen, when to sit and not do the busy work I did in her apartment to make the time pass more quickly — washing her coffee cups, straightening the newspapers, filling the cat's dish and cleaning his box. "Stop fussing," Alice would say. "I want to talk." If she were in a rage about her overcooked lunch, or some real or imagined insult from another resident, or her errant son "who never comes to see me," even though he was just there, I'd juggle the prospects of redirecting the conversation. Was it time to bring up last night's Red Sox game, or was it better to take a slow walk down the hall to "empty the garbage," which didn't need emptying but bought us both a time-out if she or I were ready to blow.

I had little training for this juggling job, but I volunteered because Alice needed it done and because my husband needed a break. John, who is an only child, had been the prime juggler since 2000, the year Alice turned 80, and we'd moved her out of her Connecticut home into a one-floor condo near us. As her health problems got worse and the breast cancer, which had been in remission, attacked her spine, we moved her into a terrific assisted-living facility in town.

But no matter how attentive the nurses and aides were, or how creative the activity directors were, nothing could fill the deepening mental void in Alice's life. She wanted us there, preferably constantly. She also needed us there to take her to a growing list of medical appointments. An assisted-living shuttle service provided transportation, but Alice needed one of us in the examining room to take notes, ask questions, and remember what the doctor prescribed.

John's work schedule was more flexible than mine, and his office was closer to home, so he'd been handling just about all of it — appointments for routine ear cleanings, colds, rashes, checkups, broken teeth, pain spasms in the joints, dizziness, soaring blood pressure, and chest tightness. There were trips to the emergency room, blood tests, x-rays, MRIs, and oncology treatments. There was a vertebroplasty to cement her crumbling spine and a heart catheterization to make sure nothing was blocked. There were stops at the drugstore on the way home from the doctor appointments and the placement of more medication on Alice's crowded kitchen counter. There were tearful phone calls to John after he went back to work because anything new panicked her.

He would go back over and calm her down, as he did when she couldn't find her keys, her purse, her glasses, or her teeth, or when she couldn't remember how her furniture had come to be "in this place," or when she was convinced her sleeping cat was dead.

Retirement meant it was my turn to take on more of that. My idea, not John's. He didn't want me to get bogged down. "She's my mother," he said.

"Our mother," I said, convinced the invigorating new retirement life would make this family responsibility easy.

It didn't. It couldn't. Having time to be there could only intensify the experience. And, sitting at the Valentine's Day lunch with four people who were hard of hearing, I did want to slip out the back door and run away. Alice had just announced she was going upstairs to get her cat so he could "meet the company." The cat wanted to run away, too, when she tried to carry him out of the apartment. Mr. Moto, who had come from a shelter, was not a social guy, and he spent a lot of time under the bed. Alice adored him, and we were glad the place allowed pets, but nobody expected him for lunch.

I suggested she bring down a photo of him. She did but was furious with me the rest of the day for telling her what to do.

You have a *car?*" one of the women at the lunch table asked as Alice started to pass around the photo. "What kind of car?"

"A cat," said Alice. "I have a cat."

"I don't drive," said the woman.

Would I get that way? Was this a preview? Would I be in bed by 7:30 at night and downstairs by 7:30 in the morning to stake out a good seat in the lobby so I could watch people come and go? Would I count visitors and keep score? Would I say, "Alice had three today *and* her son"?

A well-groomed, white-haired man confirmed my fears as I walked down the hall with the garbage that didn't need emptying.

"Hi," I said. "How's it going?"

"Hello there," he said, looking me over, looking hopeful. "You just move in? I can show you around."

Was it time to go blonde and rethink Botox? Was it my aging self, or Alice's, that prompted her to keep urging me to make an appointment with the assisted-living hairdresser? "She's really good, and you should do something with that clump that sticks up in the back." I'd feel for the cowlick, picture myself under a dryer in curlers, smelling of a fresh, tight perm, loose slippers on my feet, polyester all over my body.

Would I eventually sit in silent fury in a darkening apartment, the automotive ads held pointedly in front of my face?

"So, you've been off having a high old time for yourself again," Alice would say. "Must be nice." She would tell me she was going to buy a car so she could "get the hell out of here and do what I want."

"Where would you like to go?" I'd ask.

"Anywhere. And Johnny had no right to give my car away. I've been driving since I was 16."

"I know it's hard."

"You don't know. Nobody knows."

Sometimes I'd sit out in the parking lot, listening to the radio, because going in was too depressing. Sometimes I'd stand in our kitchen and yell, "She is driving me absolutely flippin' nuts!" So much for the Mother Teresa award.

"What are you doing today?" Alice would ask during our visits, like a girlfriend, urging me to come to the afternoon sing-along.

"Stuff," I'd say. "I've got to do lots of stuff."

"Oh, pooh," she'd say. "You're retired."

We'd stare at each other, and she'd wait for me to weaken. Sometimes I did. Sometimes the juggler would remember that I hadn't been to an event since the craft fair, or the fashion show, or the program with the actress doing a historical tour of the White House. I'd promise to come early so we'd get seats. And the singing, no matter how off-key or corny, did make me feel good. Such is the magic of music.

Alice's big laugh made me feel good. When she'd come back from a meal and say that she and her tablemates "got the giggles and laughed like fools, but I can't remember why," I was glad for the joke, whatever it was, and laughed too.

I felt good when she became a star in the charcoal drawing class and, amazingly, could recite Longfellow's "Psalm of Life" in a poetry session. She'd remembered it from high school.

She considered the smallest favors the greatest gifts — drying her feet, helping her put on a pair of socks, finding comfortable shoes. The years I'd spent trying to write clever sentences and playing with ideas seemed remote and antiseptic by comparison. The perfect adjective could not touch corns gently, wrap the towel around her shoulders to rub the wetness away, or help her put on her pants one leg at a time.

Alice lived primarily in the present and often seemed to be

seeing things for the first time. The clothes in her closet surprised her. The photographs on her shelves seemed new, and she'd hold the school picture of her grandniece and say, "Who brought me this lovely picture of Sarah?" She would keep her birthday presents in their boxes for months and reopen them many times, delighting in each one and the person who gave it to her.

The arrival of dinnertime at 4:30 could be a stunner, as could the day of the week, or the season. "I thought it was winter," she'd say, looking out at the greenery. "But it's beautiful."

"Susan, you're here!" she'd say on her happy, high-energy days, her large blue-green eyes bright as I opened her apartment door. The visits could be numbingly routine for me, but she could feel the joy of the moment as an unexpected treat. And wasn't that a perfect way to greet a loved one? People so easily take each other for granted, forgetting to hold dear what they assume is forever, forgetting to think, if not shout out loud, "Wow! It's you!"

Alice's joy and energy evaporated as that last year moved into real winter. Her last happy time was Thanksgiving with the family in a local restaurant that was wheelchair-accessible. We rolled her in on a blustery, rainy day. She hugged everyone and raised her wineglass, but with effort, feeling its weight.

The next day, she fell as she was leaving the dining room in the assisted-living facility. By Christmas, she was in a nursing home, part of that sad lineup of wheelchairs in the hall near the nursing station — the place Alice called "the train station."

The home was considered a "good" one, but it was a bad experience, and I think most nursing homes are. We found the Medicare/Medicaid bureaucracy impenetrable. With only a few sunny exceptions, the poorly paid nursing aides resented being there and showed it. When I asked one woman to help me get Alice into the bathroom, she turned and walked away. When Alice was throwing up at lunch, I caught the vomit in her napkin and looked around for help. The aides shrugged and ignored the situation.

The doctors were friendly, but in a condescending way, focused on dispensing drugs to keep people quiet. They were treating a population that, for the most part, was never going back home. Residents were strapped to alarmed chairs in many cases, as Alice was, and they yelled and kicked, as Alice did, until medicated into docility. The nurses empathized with the patients and families, as nurses usually do. They gave hugs easily and tried to help. But they were overworked and understaffed and, I think, as frustrated as we were with the rules, the aides, and the doctors.

We were grateful Alice didn't linger there and that she had made her wishes plain years before when she was lucid — no feeding tubes, no machines, no resuscitation. But even though we had her signature on papers attesting to those wishes, had signed her up with hospice, and had "Do Not Resuscitate" and "Do Not Hospitalize" on her chart, she was rushed to the emergency room two days before she died. An inexperienced nurse, worried about Alice's erratic blood pressure, called an ambulance after consulting with one of the house doctors by phone. Perhaps he was as preoccupied as he usually looked while making his rounds. Perhaps he was watching *ER*.

In those last seven weeks, I revised my previous definition of "depressing." Alice communicated less and less and got to where she could repeat only a few phrases, and eventually she would just point and babble. "Lo and behold," she'd say as she moved her hands back and forth along the tray on her wheelchair. "Lo and behold."

She always knew us but still looked surprised to see us. "Johnny!" she'd say in slurred speech, barely understandable. "How did you find me?" She must have figured that if she didn't know where she was, nobody else could know either.

But, even then, there was still music. I'd roll Alice into the activity room and we'd sing along with the guitar and banjo and keyboard players. Sometimes I'd dance around Alice's wheelchair, making her laugh as I held her hand, pretending she was my partner.

One day I heard singing as I got out of the elevator, and I saw that the people lined up at "the train station" were providing their own entertainment in a blend of beautiful sopranos, basses, and tenors. Joe, who was about 20 years younger than the rest and who had a flirtation going with Alice, was leading the group in a chorus of "Bicycle Built for Two." I joined in, did a soft-shoe dance along the wheelchair line, and sat next to Alice.

We sang "You Wore a Tulip," "Row, Row, Row Your Boat," "Michael Row the Boat Ashore," "Clementine," and "Oh Susannah." We were loud. The nurses joined in. We laughed. We told stories about when we sang the songs in camp and in school. We felt a little reckless, as though we might be breaking a rule, and kind of hoped we were. That Friday afternoon was a gift.

Three weeks later, on another Friday afternoon, February 2 at 3:15, Alice died in her sleep. But again, miraculously it seemed, there was music. As John and I held her hands in the room with the soft green walls, the door closed, we could hear an entertainer in the activity room singing, "Hail, Hail, the Gang's All Here," followed by "Don't Be Cruel," "Stay Until It's Time for

You to Go," and, finally, "You Are My Special Angel." That, too, was a gift.

The nurses came in and hugged us and cried with us. But the room felt more peaceful than sad, the passage a relief. "She's free now," we said, and I looked up at the ceiling, as though she might be there, watching. An image came to me from a day in the fall of 1986, shortly after Alice had retired from her state job. I could see her spinning around in the living room, her brightly colored shift making a swirl as she clapped her hands, did a little dance, and sang out, "Weeeeeeeeeee! No more work. I feel so free. So free!"

CHAPTER 8

Paradise

The names were swimming together in a real-estate marketing fog. I had taken too many tours, read too many brochures, seen too many ads, and lusted after the amenities in the Promised Land of retirement perfection:

WELCOME TO STONEBRIDGE POINT FARM
VILLAGE ON THE POND

… AT THE LANDING

… IN THE WOODS

… OVER THE HILL

… AROUND THE BEND

An Active Adult Over 55 Community
Where the Bocce Never Stops

And You Live the Lifestyle You Deserve
But Probably Can't Afford

Why was I doing this to myself? Because the Promised Land was there, and the real-estate market hadn't tanked yet. And because I had the time. Oh, that old devil, time, letting me wander off again, refusing to call "Foul!" the way he did when a boss writing paychecks expected productivity. Now I expected productivity of myself but wasn't quite sure what it was.

Was it productive to think about where John and I would live in 10 or 20 years? Was it productive and smart to get on a waiting list for a maintenance-free, all-on-one-floor home in what John called "one of those places," making it sound like Geezer Acres? I didn't want to be like his mother, who refused to plan, and who would have fallen down her basement stairs if we hadn't forced her to move at age 80. There were no children to get us moving, so we'd better stay ahead of the arthritis, better admit there would come a time when the laundry room would seem like a long way down.

"That is so depressing," said my husband, whose home office is next to the laundry room. "My head is not even close to thinking that way."

The working man in his fifties faced the retired woman in her sixties, the retired woman who was compulsive about details and had to be at the airport three hours before the plane took off, the woman who made lists of lists and plans for plans.

"It's not like these are nursing homes or assisted-living facilities," I told him. "These are beautiful homes." Friends in Massachusetts had moved to "one of those places" and loved the fleet of clubhouses, tennis courts, pools, and activities. Friends in

Maryland had chosen a smaller, quieter development where they would be free to travel and let somebody else mow the lawn and shovel snow. Why not consider the options for when we reached an age we never thought we'd reach?

"What's wrong with where we are?"

Nothing was wrong. Now. I was itchy about later. Well, maybe I was itchy about now, too, because the 1970s split ranch-style home with the scratched harvest gold Formica counters and small rooms was looking a little tired. Moving would be an adventure, and an adventure would be good to have while we could still have one or two.

Was that another depressing thought?

My husband walked out to the porch and stared at the tall grass we'd hired a kid to mow, a kid who was usually a week or so behind. "I don't want to think about it," John said. "Not yet."

I'm not sure what I wanted to think about — staying young or getting old? We'd been in our house for 20 years. When we moved there, I wrote a piece for the *Boston Globe* magazine about the joys of a "starter" home, the magic of bonding with that first house, which is like a marriage in the way eager new owners look beyond imperfections to focus on the possibilities. We did some remodeling, but it was still basically a two-floor house with narrow doorways and a shaky pull-down set of stairs leading to an attic crawl space. How long do we want to make *that* trip? We never considered the question in 1987, when a house with crumbling shingles on an acre of crabgrass seemed like Paradise.

Do people see more clearly with age or do they just get near-sighted? Was I taking a rational 20/20 view of the obvious or being seduced by flashy "finisher" homes, too eager to trade old dreams and decades of memories for pricey practicalities?

I flipped through the glossy pages of *Where to Retire* magazine, which is one big advertisement for all the places on the planet designed for the "active adult." That's shorthand for someone over 55 who won't admit how much ibuprofen it takes to play tennis.

The active adults waved at me in full-page color photos taken at the net, the pool, on the fairway, in sculpture classes, from square dances, and on bicycle rides with mountains or marinas in the background, sometimes with mountains *and* marinas. They were often seated at tables, drinking wine. "It's like being on vacation all the time," they told me in quotes written across a photograph of a cloudless sky.

They told me the reward for a well-managed career was party time without the kids, without the worries, Paradise. It waited in the Sun Belt, in the middle of the country, and on the coasts of a graying America. It was going up everywhere developers develop land for my generation, and for the people just behind, or just ahead of it.

I imagined packing up the Toyota and heading west, a senior pioneer joining the big barbecue in Arizona or Texas. "Howdy, Pardner. I'm from Hingham. Nice boots." Or maybe I'd just go down Route 3 to the Cape and still feel like Daniel Boone, because the Cape is a place where I always get lost.

They were gorgeous, these active adults in their spacious condos and houses, where the great rooms flowed from the kitchen to the family room with the plasma TV, and on out to the white wicker porch. They told me I would love the granite countertops, track lighting, ceiling paddle fans, patios, activities coordinators, potluck dinners in the pub, and the formal restaurant with the white tablecloths. They told me I wouldn't ever chip ice off the front steps again, and in spring the mulch would appear like velvet magic under exquisitely pruned shrubbery.

I felt the mighty magnet of consumerism yanking me out of harvest gold and loose faux brick linoleum into the blazing sun of the word "new." I flew from a low-ceilinged lifestyle, which does not allow for paddle fans because they could decapitate someone, and rose into the airy space of cathedral beams and skylights.

I was atwitter at the prospect of "walking trails," never mind that in my current home I could go outside and stroll down the sidewalk. A sidewalk was not a trail. I knew where the sidewalk went. It went to the corner. But a trail, well . . . a trail was something else, something exotic, something new.

I could have a garden plot, too, and built-in bookshelves, and a washer/dryer combo off the kitchen, and walk-in closets the size of an office. I could have anything I wanted in Paradise.

I headed out to find it, answering the call of the cul-de-sac despite nearly four decades of absorbing New England culture, where older is better and where it's not really old unless it came over on the Mayflower. I headed out despite reading Thoreau and Emerson and knowing that neither of them needed amenities or an adventure beyond their own minds. "I have traveled a good deal in Concord," said Thoreau.

I traveled in the state of Massachusetts looking at bad deals. Two hours south of my driveway was a STONEBRIDGE POINT FARM VILLAGE ON THE POND AT THE LANDING that was also a PORT with two lakes and an ocean.

"If you buy now you get a three-season porch free," said the salesperson. "That's a $22,800 value at no cost to you."

She was a pleasant, perky lady in her forties, and she told

me she couldn't wait until she was old enough to live there. She made me wish somebody had carded me on the way in.

The condos were lovely, many bigger than our house. The outside pool was heated. The golf course rolled on and on. The bocce and tennis courts looked new. The landscaping was perfect, not a weed allowed. The indoor pool was part of a fitness complex with personal trainers, aerobics, and yoga rooms. There was a library, a computer room, and meeting space for clubs that sewed, quilted, cooked, read, or talked.

And yet I felt uneasy, trapped, or about to be. I felt like Pinocchio getting the pitch for Pleasure Island. The feeling came partly from knowing there was no such thing as a free porch. Anybody offering one was probably getting desperate in an uncertain market and just might be making up the cost somewhere less obvious — on the roof, perhaps, or in the wiring or the plumbing.

The feeling also came from a sense of walking among the cloned. The magazine ads, Web tours, and DVD promos never focused on a vista of sameness. But standing on a street that looked pretty much like every other street, where condos — starting at around $460,000 (plus taxes and fees) — were built four across with identical driveways, front doors, and garages, I wondered if people had trouble remembering which unit was theirs. Did they drop bread crumbs out to the security gate to find their way? Could they hear their neighbors behind those exquisite shared façades and walls?

I asked if the units were well soundproofed. The saleslady paused and said the walls were constructed with the best soundproofing materials available to the builder.

Uh-oh. Could this be where they buried the free porch?

"Will I hear noise?"

She paused again, perhaps prompted by her own Jiminy Cricket. "You'll hear noise," she said.

I hated noise and had heard enough of it in apartments in my twenties and thirties. I treasured the privacy of our home walls that transmitted no television laugh tracks, sub-woofer vibrations, exercise-machine clunks, late-night remodeling, temper tantrums, or growling dogs.

But wasn't everything in life a trade-off? Maybe I could learn to sacrifice uniqueness and privacy for convenience. How badly did I want or need convenience, and would it ultimately seem *in*convenient? My head was starting to ache. Paradise in person was work, especially on a sweltering September day.

I drove on, visiting a STONEBRIDGE POINT FARM VILLAGE ON THE POND AT THE LANDING with three condos across, and another with two. I visited condo units in what looked like huge apartment houses, where the average age of the residents was 75, and where security personnel knocked on the door to make sure residents were still alive in the morning. There were no noise guarantees in any of them. Maybe some of the 75-year-olds simply turned down their hearing aids.

I visited developments that were only partially developed and looked deserted. Were all the active adults out being active? Had the EPA discovered a toxic waste dump under the swimming pool?

The rumor in one town was that the units had sprouted mold in the development billed as having "the best of New England-style architecture." I called the builder and got a sunny voice saying "It's a beautiful day at STONEBRIDGE POINT FARM VILLAGE ON THE POND AT THE LANDING."

Not really, I told him, because the place I saw had bulldozers standing around, lots of dirt piles, models with locked doors, and nobody in the sales office. He gave me another number, which was a recording where I left a message but got no callback. The sunny guy sent me a customer-satisfaction survey and put me on the mailing list. The people who didn't answer the phone sent a form letter that said "Your name has been added to our interest list" and suggested I take virtual tours on their Web site. The tours did not feature mold.

I drove to a STONEBRIDGE POINT FARM VILLAGE ON THE POND AT THE LANDING that sold single-family homes. No shared walls and presumably no mold. Could this be the answer? Does anybody remember the question?

The place described itself as "New England's biggest and best active adult community." It was off a country road with farm stands and cows. It took an hour to find it. I forgot what town I was in. The security gate was open and had no guard. The sales-people were clustered in the back room of the office, speaking in low voices. A sign on the door said Employees Only Beyond This Point. I cleared my throat and waved, but they didn't look up. I busied myself reading a long list of resale homes in the $200,000 range. The list hung across from a sign offering people a $1,000 shopping spree if they bought within the next four weeks. Money Given at the Closing, it said.

Uh-oh.

"Are you all set?" a woman asked, annoyed that she had been forced to emerge from the back room. Were they playing poker back there?

"I just got here," I told her.

She handed me an information packet and pointed to the door. "The models are out back. It's a self-guided tour."

That should have told me everything I needed to know, but I looked anyway, wandering through three model homes furnished to look as though the residents had just stepped outside — quite possibly to get away from their furniture. An eat-in kitchen with a large table abutted a dining room with a large table. A tiny, angled living room looked as though it were being eaten by a sofa.

I felt like a trespasser opening closets and drawers. I felt watched. Maybe the people in the back room of the sales office had placed hidden cameras behind the pictures and were taking notes as I frowned at a thin, beige, wall-to-wall rug that would be gray in six months. Maybe they wanted to make sure I didn't ignore the sign on a toilet that said Do Not Use.

Radios were playing in two models, and I wanted to turn them off. The third model was too quiet, and I wanted to hum, but stopped, remembering the cameras behind the pictures. The great-room concept wasn't quite flowing here, even though the house looked large from the outside. The space felt tight and sterile, and I needed air.

I visited the recreation areas, which also felt squeezed together: pool right next to tennis, bocce, shuffleboard, and horseshoe pit. What would happen if everybody recreated at once? The outside pool was small, and the indoor pool had a stagnant, filmy look. A resident came by as I was studying the water and said that buying there was "the best move we ever made." There was nothing she didn't like. "And the kids can't move in with us," she added, making the thumbs-up sign. "Against the rules."

I drove around and kept seeing the same houses over and over again. They were built on cement slabs and looked as though they were shipped in on a truck. I started hearing the old Malvina Reynolds song, "Little Boxes," but with new lyrics. It was sung by The Over-55 Active Adult Chorus, and each singer was making the thumbs-up sign:

Giant boxes on the hillside.
Giant glitzy new developments.
And they cost way more than ticky-tacky.
And they all look just the same.

I wanted to go home, wanted to be like Dorothy and click the red slippers together in the gray Toyota. But I could only turn the key and move slowly in the rush-hour traffic, a trip made longer after a few wrong turns and more cows. Nothing against cows, but the countryside was starting to look like Fargo.

Had I expected too much? Was I getting cranky looking for perfection? On another day, in a different mood, would I embrace the prospect of living in a giant box? Would I think I was in Phoenix? On another day, in a different mood, I might seek out different alternatives — buying a Victorian house with friends, joining a senior commune, or signing on to a service network similar to Cambridge at Home or Beacon Hill Village, which helped people with errands, chores, and transportation so they could stay in their homes.

Staying in my home seemed like a swell idea. I drove down our street with renewed appreciation for the mishmash that created a neighborhood's wonderful non-style. There were Capes, colonials, split-levels, one-levels; the grand next to the tiny; some with dirt driveways, some with blacktop; some with attached garages, freestanding garages, or no garages. There were condos, too, and a brook, and a swamp, and down at the end of the road an entrance to a state park. It is a street shaped by nature and individuals who discovered what was uniquely their own.

I walked up the steps of our squat, boring, split-level ranch and remembered the first time I saw it and how big it had seemed compared to a one-bedroom apartment. I remembered how John and I ripped up the ugly gold wall-to-wall rug late one night on sudden inspiration and stood there amazed at the wood floors hiding beneath it. I remembered painting the dark woodwork white, remembered the houseful of friends over for St. Patrick's Day parties, the brunches and cookouts. I remembered watching my friend Ellen's girls make colored chalk drawings on the driveway and watching them grow up in short summer visits over the years. I remembered cooking our first Thanksgiving turkey for the relatives and opening presents that first Christmas morning. Every year since, we have hung up a big, white, corny Hallmark ornament decorated with cardinals and the date: 1987.

I thought of my grandfather buying what he called "my little house" back in the 1950s. He dreamed of retiring there as he rented it to tenants while continuing to work and live in his tailor shop a few miles away. The little house was very little, a one-bedroom with a kitchen, living room, and bathroom. It was on San Diego Avenue in Cleveland, diagonally across from my family's house. Grandpa worked six days a week and took the bus to join us for Sunday dinner after he mopped up the shop and got his work ready for Monday morning. "Someday," he'd say, looking over at the house he thought of as Paradise, "I'll plant a garden and gooseberry bushes."

But a series of small strokes and a balance problem kept him from moving in. He lived with us when he retired and died in a nursing home after breaking his hip in our living room. My parents thought they'd found Paradise in Orlando, Florida, and moved down in their sixties to get away from winter after they retired — my mother had managed a bridal shop and my dad sold insurance. But they were responsible for their own maintenance in oppressive heat, and they missed their friends in Ohio. My dad died three years after they moved. My mother became more and more isolated, spending much of her day with the air-conditioning cranked up, reading or watching old movies. I've always wondered if they would have lived longer, and happier, up north with snow.

I KEEP ALL THE BROCHURES, information packets, ads, and follow-up letters from the real-estate marketing fog in a big canvas bag next to a file cabinet. Call it the later file. Call it the I'm-glad-I-looked-but-am-not-so-itchy-anymore file. Call it the my-husband-often-knows-my-mind-before-I-do file.

The bag has swelled even as the housing market collapsed. Realtors have sent "deal of a lifetime" e-mails, notices of "red-tag sales," and "last chance to save" postcards. They've promised to sell our house and have invited us to "meet and greet" parties. There's a guy who sends me his picture. He wears a frozen smile and looks scared. I wonder if he lives in a place with a free porch.

One afternoon, long after the bag had gathered dust, the phone rang. It was a salesperson from Arizona who wanted John and me to "come out and spend a few days on the ranch as our guests." I told her I'd given up ranching.

"You have no interest in moving to Arizona?" she asked, surprised that I could say that after viewing her company's DVD promo.

"None."

"Do you think you might be interested sometime in the next year?"

"Not gonna happen."

"All right, then," she said, her voice never losing its sweetness. "We'll take you right off our mailing list."

Good-bye, Arizona. Good-bye, STONEBRIDGE POINT FARM VILLAGE ON THE POND AT THE LANDING. We'll stay right here in our split-level ranch ON THE BROOK AT THE SWAMP. We'll keep sharing lilacs with the older couple next door. We'll keep talking to the cute kids who live in the house on the other side of us, enjoying their giggles as they jump in their plastic wading pool or play tag. We'll stay limber, watch ourselves on the steps, and live with the Formica.

Does Paradise exist? Only if you don't chase after it.

CHAPTER 9

The Age Thing

The kid on the Red Line train stood to offer me his seat. He was ageless youth, somewhere between 16 and 30. I was youthless age, somewhere between his mother and his grandmother. I thanked him for the kind gesture, but declined.

"Please," he insisted. "It's okay."

I was carrying a backpack, wearing sandals, and had a solid, confident grip on the pole. Obviously, the kid didn't recognize fitness.

"I'm fine," I told him. "I need to stretch. Spend a lot of time in the car. You sit."

"Are you sure?" he asked, holding his position between up and down. His mother, or grandmother, or both of them had trained him well. I wanted to deprogram him. What kind of question was "Are you sure?" Did I look like somebody who didn't know if she was fine? I smiled, declined again, sucked in my stomach, and tried not to think about sore arches.

A woman with a toddler got on at the next stop, and the young man was gracious once again, proving that I was the one who was obsessing about age, not he. But that didn't make the situation any less irritating. The woman with the toddler was grateful and sat, giving the young man a simple "thank you." She was also an ageless youth and felt no compulsion to explain her driving habits, suck in her stomach, or sweat the possibility of looking like a retirement cliché. For her, the seat was just a seat, not a categorization, not a decision to be on one side or the other of a generational dateline that divided people into those who felt entitled to age perks and those who didn't want to admit they were eligible.

The kid wasn't the first person ever to offer me a seat, but he was the first since I'd retired, and he pricked the insecurity about exactly where I belonged on the big subway car of life. Someday I might cross the dateline with grace and sit quietly in hastily offered space. Someday I might welcome an assist crossing a street and be philosophical about obvious infirmity, knowing that acceptance is wisdom. But right now I need to prove I'm not there yet. Right now I'd rather stand, just like I'd rather pay full price at the movie theatre because asking for the senior discount feels like something my grandmother would have done.

Grandma saved used tea bags. She let them shrivel up and turn yellow in the spoon rest on the stove until she boiled water for another cup, which never tasted as good as the first. Used tea bags helped her through the Great Depression, and she saw no need to start giving Mr. Lipton extra pennies just because times were good. My grandmother bought day-old bread. She clipped coupons out of the newspaper, neatly, and kept them in stacks on the kitchen table. She opened bank accounts to get toasters. She would have gone nuts with an AARP card.

I have an AARP card but keep it in the wallet behind the AAA card and hope nobody will ask to see it. I don't object to bargains and use the AAA membership for discounts on hotels and car rentals because doing so is age-neutral and comes with no psychological baggage. I'm fine with coupons that arrive in the mail and don't have to be clipped and with two-for-one midweek specials at restaurants as long as they're not called "early bird." I have no problem with sidewalk sales or cheap chicken in the supermarket as long as there is no sign out front saying "Today is senior-discount day!"

It's having to declare myself "one of them" that's the croaker, especially in a movie line while standing in front of a cool couple who, while not exactly ageless youth, do carry their fifties or sixties like 40-year-olds. She's about a size six with perfect hair. He has a hint of gray at the temples and looks like a runner. They've probably made a million in something recession-proof. They've hiked Mt. Kilimanjaro, and they have sex every night. Maybe they've had sex on Mt. Kilimanjaro. Whoever they are, they are not going to see John and me play the fogy card.

John slaps the full freight on the ticket counter and says in a clear, strong voice, "Two adults, please."

Go get 'em, Tiger! Adults, yes! Okay, middle-aged adults, whatever that means. The definition is pretty loose out here in the vast, murky middle, which runs from — what? — 30- or 40-something to wherever it stops, which depends on who is counting and what the person looks like when he or she is counted.

Putting it another way, if 60 is the new 40, I'm about 43, no matter how good Lauren Hutton looked on the cover of AARP's magazine when she turned 60 and said it was the new 30. Does anyone remember what the old 30 or 40 looked like? And will 80 or 90 eventually be the new 60?

What does it mean to be "a woman of a certain age"? Is that anything over 50? And why aren't men referred to that way? Older men are usually "distinguished" or "active," never mind that people say the word "active" as though they're amazed the guy is still moving.

Anyone who receives birthday cards that make jokes about Viagra, colonoscopies, face-lifts, hearing problems, or memory lapses is probably "of a certain age" or "active." People who get cards with long poems printed inside and bluebirds flying around the stanzas should do a pulse check because they could be on their way out.

What does it mean when "a woman of a certain age" is called "Miss" in the grocery store? It was "Ma'am" for years, from about age 35 on, so much "Ma'aming" that I almost got used to it and stopped grinding my molars over it. If I'd lived in the South, I would have accepted it as a nicety from the get-go. But this is New England, where "Ma'am" rings matriarchal and is said with a hint of impatience, as though service personnel figure this customer is likely to be demanding and about to make trouble.

Around the year 2000, according to my informal observations in suburbs south of Boston, there was a Ma'am Shift. I suspect it was a marketing decision by retail executives who had finally heard the molars grinding. Memos must have been drafted, courtesy policies revamped, and the word sent out: "If they're breathing, do not call them 'Ma'am.'" Now solicitous clerks lean over their deli counters and raise their voices so that a white-haired, wizened soul gripping her shopping cart like a walker can hear the words, "May I help you, *Miss?*" The woman just ahead of her in line, who got the same treatment and credited it to an expensive dye job and a diet, controls the urge to revert to a ma'am stereotype and does not slap the clerk with a half-pound of low-fat cheese.

How old am I? How old are you? Does it matter? The answers are as much cultural as chronological and come filtered through a bombardment of messages, real or imagined.

It used to be so simple. A grown-up would lean down to tricycle level and ask the age question. The little person on the tricycle would hold up three fingers. The little person always wanted to be older than three fingers, wanted to be bigger and ready for the two-wheeler, the big kids' slide on the playground, the roller coaster at the amusement park. The little person was an individual planted firmly on a number, often tacking "and a half" onto it to make it seem larger.

Now the little person is a big person slip-sliding around on a lot of numbers. There's the basic, raw total on file with the Social Security Administration, where the government says the little person turned big is eligible to collect. But that seems like a howler of a mathematical error against the potency of Lauren Hutton and the new 30, or 40, and the promises of moisture creams that are supposed to take 10 years off any total. These ads feature presumed husbands saying, "I looked at her — and wow! I couldn't believe she was my wife. She looked so good." A debatable compliment, but it does sell cream and reinforces the belief that age comes in a jar, not a federal database.

The government's basic raw total also founders on the perception a lot of us have about being Baby Boomers, even though we were born in late or mid-1945. The official cutoff date for the start of that generation is January 1, 1946. But what's a couple of months among people who all grew up watching *Howdy Doody?* I think of us 1945 babies as trendsetters, ahead of our time, who are entitled to slide on over to the pivotal Boomer date and take a year off our raw number whenever we feel like it.

So, how old am I? Well, let's see. In addition to waltzing around the questionable federal total, I work with a psychological base number. That's a mental tally that best reflects the current psyche. Right now the psychological base is somewhere around 50, a good, solid, believable number that's mature, yet still tethered to the forties, which used to sound mature but now sounds young. The psychological base works as a kind of meditation, anchoring the gestalt, particularly on a bad day when some busybody has suggested a trip to the Senior Center for easy stretching classes that people do while holding onto chairs. There have been other psychological base numbers over the years — 40, 35, 21. Eventually 60 will become a base, and then 65, but not until 50 is the new 20.

I also have a running daily number. This one rises and falls like the Dow Jones Industrial Average, fluctuating with the variables of chance meetings on subways, assumptions about physical capability, the intensity of winter weather, too much exercise, not enough exercise, fat days, new slacks, fresh haircuts, bad light, good light, and a sudden jolting glimpse of a stranger with too many chins wearing my clothes in a department-store mirror. I have studied this stranger and thought: "That woman should never wear lime green," before recognizing the face and adding at least 15 years to all the numbers, including the psychological base.

I play with nostalgic and geographical numbers, too, that flip back time and make me think I'm still that little person on the tricycle, or the 16-year-old getting the driver's license, or the college graduate settling into that first New York job and apartment, or the 25-year-old transplant to 1970s Boston, feeling the January wind for the first time on the wide walks of the Prudential Center shopping area, which long ago morphed into the enclosed Copley Place.

But I still see the Pru the way it was 40 years ago, even while strolling the pedestrian bridges and being overwhelmed with Copley Place retail glitz. I see the ice-skaters, the old Pine & Print stationery store, the red, white, and blue Brigham's sandwich and ice cream shop, and the apothecary with all those perfumes.

Out on Boylston Street, my twenties yank me back into Mass Camera to buy my first 35-mm, a used Miranda. They plunk me into Ken's Restaurant for an enormous late-night corned beef sandwich with a side of chips when nobody cared about cholesterol, and then into Paperback Booksmith to browse the shelves until closing.

Downtown on Washington Street, I see past the stripped façades of a stalled construction project that make the shopping district look like a bomb site. I focus on the Filene's Department Store clock, still clinging to the side of what's left of the building, and feel the hot crush of a bargain-basement stampede racing toward hundreds of sweaters unloaded on tables. I can still see the ghost of Filene's competitor, Jordan Marsh, and the lesser threats of Raymond's, Woolworth's, and Stearn's, with its creaky cagelike elevators that would probably result in a lawsuit today.

I think the Lechmere appliance store lives because the name is still on the front of trolley cars going to what is now a Cambridge shopping mall. But it is a Lechmere-less Lechmere.

I look at the pay phones along the edge of Boston Common and feel the coins in my pocket as I start to call apartment-rental agents about studios available for under $500 a month. I walk through South Station and feel the weight of the now-disappeared wooden doors that I can barely push open into the ferocity of the Blizzard of '78. I've been on an eight-hour train ride coming back from a *Boston Globe* assignment in New York. Miraculously, the *Globe's* cab service gets there, one of a half-dozen cars on the road that night. I walk to the cab, bent over so the wind won't knock me down. The snow is flying sideways and feels like needles on the skin.

How old am I? Old enough to remember when cuisine in Boston meant fried clams, when the Red Sox were cursed and the Patriots didn't exist, when it was all Route 128, not I-95 and I-93 at the same time, when the waterfront was warehouses and rats, when Faneuil Hall Marketplace had the bright bags of Lucy's Canvas instead of the Gap, when there was a Bank of Boston and it lived here with John Hancock Life Insurance, and when Betty parked her white Rolls-Royce illegally outside her piano-bar restaurant of the same name, and the car was loaded with tickets. And she got a story in the paper when she paid them.

All gone? Was it really another century?

How old am I? The years are tallied in so many ways it's easy to lose track. I go to retiree dinners, book signings, and funerals, and measure time according to the OPW Index. That stands for "other people's wrinkles."

"Can't be Joe," I think, staring across the room at the old

man talking to other old men who used to be young men when we started working together at the newspaper. "Strange how they have aged and I haven't." This thought is quickly followed by another: "If that can't be Joe, is somebody staring across the room, thinking, 'That can't be Susan'?"

How many years ago was it that we were all young? Lots. As a friend said when she invited me to speak to her college journalism class: "Don't tell them you were at the newspaper 32 years. That's more time than they've been alive, and they won't be able to relate."

Fellow retirees and I have reached the age of "You're looking great!" Or as Billy Crystal says, "MAHvelous!" That's what we tell each other through hugs and air kisses, often imitating Billy, no matter how high the OPW Index is or how much hair has vanished since the last time we saw each other. "You're looking great!" "Hey, doesn't he look great?" "It sure is great to feel great!" The word is our mantra, our validation, proof that we know what to do with all that free time.

Working people also feel obliged to say that to us, but when they do, it has an edge that's part envy and part superiority. The employed know they are busting their buns and think the retired are merely sitting on theirs. "You look great," they say, thinking to themselves, "And why shouldn't you look great? You've got nothing to do."

How old am I? Sometimes I forget and forget the ages of friends, which never used to happen at 10, 16, or 21. But now I have to stop and think: was she 60 last year or is it this year? Did I send this card already?

What day is it? What year is it? Am I too old for the roller coaster? If you know, don't tell me.

→ CHAPTER 10 ←

The Little Housewife

I worry that I'm turning into June Cleaver. The kiss at the door in the morning. The kiss and the question at night: "How was your day, Dear?" I ask it while stirring a pot, checking inside the oven, tasting the mustard sauce. Sometimes I wear an apron. No dress, low heels, or pearls, but clean slacks and a fresh top instead of the clothes worn since breakfast. Sometimes I change earrings.

I never changed earrings after coming home from work. Just put on sweats and slippers, and blobbed out. There was no need to look put together, to present the dinner as an accomplishment. When I had a job and a commute, dinner was basic sustenance, taken at no particular time, easily eaten out, or arriving in a box labeled "Pizza." John often got home first and cooked fish because fish was fast. It was a matter of practicality, this meal known as dinner, a non-gender-specific bit of business taken care of in the kitchen before we collapsed in the living room and traded sections of the local afternoon newspaper.

Now John reads the paper as I finish making the meal,

which is usually on the table between 6:00 and 6:30. It is a meal planned that morning or sometimes the day before. Textures are considered — rice, not boiled potatoes, with chicken in honey sherry sauce because rice absorbs liquid better. Colors are coordinated — yellow squash instead of asparagus with a salad so there aren't too many greens. I focus on health and variety — chicken and fish, but not too much, and neither one two nights in a row. The occasional lamb chop makes an appearance with red wine, as does the meat loaf made with "85% lean beef," whatever that means. I put on the glasses to scrutinize the label in the store, look up "85% lean" on the Web at home, have no idea what I'm reading, and eat the meat loaf anyway.

I contemplate the pros and cons of chicken skin and wonder if it should come off, even though *Joy of Cooking* leaves it on. I look up recipes for tilapia and decide to stick with scrod. I ask another shopper in the produce department why she's buying the flat Italian parsley instead of the curly kind and she gives me a 10-minute riff on "flavor." She tells me there's "no comparison" and that once I cook with flat Italian I will never go back to curly. This seems important at two o'clock in the afternoon on a Wednesday when people with jobs are sitting at desks making money. I buy the flat Italian and don't notice any difference in taste, but keep buying it to look smart.

Parsley is my job now, or part of it. A woman at home with a husband at the office is responsible for food, as in "preparing" it from a grocery list that includes herbs. No more last-minute throwing it in the cart and cooking it tomorrow because we're too tired tonight and would rather go out. The little housewife rules the kitchen, and her once unassailable feminist self watches, confused, and sometimes appalled.

There I am on my stomach, reaching under the refrigerator with a yard stick to pull out Cheerios, nuts, ossified beans, uncooked elbow macaroni, cooked elbow macaroni, plastic bag fasteners, and grapes that have gone beyond raisins and are on their way to vinegar. I never used to care what was under there, never noticed the grease along the bottom of the stove drawer, or the tea bags that had missed the wastebasket under the sink.

There I am searching Google for the best way to clean mini-blinds. I was too busy for mini-blinds when I had an office job. I still write in an office but it's at home next to a bedroom with an unmade bed that needs attention. The work competes with corner cobwebs, nicks in the paint, dust on the lamps, spots on the glassware, messy closets, dry cleaning tickets, bills, demanding cats, the arrival of the mail truck, oil truck, or septic tank truck, the dripping faucet, the repairman, the tree guys, the snow, the rain, and the wind. It's all my department. Nobody assigns it. I take it on because it is there and I am here.

Something in the genes, the estrogen, and that sense of guilt about being free when my husband works drives me to the drugstore newsstand to buy *Woman's Day* magazine because the issue features free recipe cards. An appalled feminist self urges me to buy the *The Economist,* but I can't find it in the rack and go to the checkout line holding the magazine with the bright red February cover and the valentine cookies all over it.

I decide to make *Woman's Day* "braised pork and apple stew," but I have never purchased a pork loin and ask the meat-counter clerk at the grocery store what it is and where to find one. She gives me what I think is "the look" that working people give little housewives who are wandering around meat counters instead of going to jobs. Am I imagining this look? Over-reacting because I used to give the same look of superiority tinged with jealousy to women strolling down the street for a morning walk when I was pulling out of the driveway in business clothes?

I wonder if the dishwasher repairman is smirking when he asks, "Not working today?"

"Took the day off," I tell him, not mentioning I'll do the same with the other 364.

Does the doctor think I'm boring? I've been his patient for almost 30 years, and for most of those years he's asked about the newspaper. "How's life at the *Boston Globe*," he'd ask, wanting to know the gossip, what I was working on, and when it would be published.

Now he says, "What are you doing to keep yourself busy?"

"Working at home," I answer in what feels like a strong freelance-writer-person voice.

"Doing little housewifey things?" he asks absently, focusing on my file. Has he seen me in the drugstore buying *Woman's Day*?

"I write," I tell him, hoping that didn't sound as defensive as it felt.

"But you don't have a job," he says, pleasantly, not hearing what I'm hearing, not aware that his patient is becoming invisible. "You don't leave the house and go to work."

My feminist self wants to go into kung fu mode. *Kick, kick, chop, chop! These hands are weapons!* Such rage is why Betty Friedan started the revolution. And why I joined it. But I leave the doctor's office without breaking anything, without trying to verbalize the frustration of being a demoted modern woman, redefined by the old rules.

Funny how retirement can zap a raised consciousness right back to the Stone Age. It's a little like the WABAC machine on the old *Rocky and Bullwinkle Show*.

"Golly, Mr. Peabody, where are we going today?"

"To the laundry room, Sherman. Circa 1955."

And there I am, trying to get those stains whiter than white. I even try to iron John's shirts. Once. There are eight of them, Oxford cloth. They came in a wrinkled pack from a catalogue company. Why send new, clean shirts to the dry cleaner just for pressing? We have a steam iron in the house, and my mother taught me how to use it.

Mom was fast with the iron and with the sprinkler bottle, too, before she had steam. She'd douse my father's white shirts with water from an old catsup bottle fit with a silver top full of holes. The silver top came from the dime store "notions" department. All the mothers had them. In summer, after sprinkling the shirts, she'd roll each one into a ball and keep them in a bag in the refrigerator to prevent mildew until she ironed.

None of the mothers back then would have thought of taking shirts to the dry cleaner. They washed with ancient wringer machines before automatic rinse-and-spin cycles, and they line-dried in summer and winter before gas and electric dryers. Then they got out the ironing board.

"You always start with the collar," my mother instructed in her pay-attention-or-you'll-be-sorry-voice on the day I graduated from doing handkerchiefs. After the collar came the yoke, followed by the cuffs and sleeves. Next she moved the iron expertly down the placket, maneuvering quickly around the buttons without scorching them. She finished with broad, strong sweeps up and down the sides and back, the ironing board creaking as she leaned into the task.

I can see her as I stand in my laundry room 50 years later, listening to the iron hiss. I can hear her after an hour passes and not quite two shirts are pressed, and not very well: "Good God, girl! Give me that iron and let's get on with it."

She had practice. I had a job. And when she got a job after 17 years of marriage, my dad was wearing polyester.

It's a different time now. I don't have to prove anything. And yet, I study catalogues of household gadgets as though there will be a quiz. I fuss with dryer lint and worry about the possibility of a vent fire, fixating on one catalogue that warns, "Think you removed all the lint from your dryer? Think again, before it's too late." I send away for a 10-foot dryer-cleaning brush with directions, written in Taiwan and not quite translated into English:

"With this brush you be pushing the accumulated lint out of the vent. There, if you have a long vent pipe it may be necessary to separate a joint to allow removal of the lint dislodged by the brush. . . . Gain access to your vent pipe by carefully disconnecting the vent from the dryer. It is usually necessary to slide the dryer out of the way to accomplish this, so use care. CAUTION — do not damage gas or electrical connections while performing any of these procedures."

The brush remains sealed in its plastic shipping bag, gathering dust, and, occasionally, lint. It sits next to a 42-inch "flexi-hose," purchased as a companion gadget to the brush and designed to be a vacuum cleaner attachment that can "clean deep down into the lint trap." I haven't been able to make it do much, certainly nothing close to the performance described in the testimonial included with the directions. S. Beinar of Tucson,

Arizona, writes: "I clean my lint trap every load and I never imagined that the build-up in my dryer was that bad. I will say a lot came out of that dryer and now I get my work done in less time."

Something to strive for, although John tells me to stop sweating the boring stuff. He has to fight me for the job of washing the grit off the bathroom walls to prep them for painting. "Don't mess with that on your day off," I tell him, mad at myself for not taking care of it during the week. "But I want to mess with it," he insists, noting that the job needs his muscle and height, and that he lives here too and does do windows.

I laugh, but on some primal level, still feel inadequate. Ancient impulses trigger the synapses, stereotypes pervade the intellect, subliminal messages on the big billboard in the brain flash commercials for bleach. A directive floats up out of the primordial soup (no doubt, cooked from scratch) and reaches across the epochs: *Husband goes out to hunt wild beast; wife stays home and pounds underwear on rock.*

SINCE THE DAY WE WERE MARRIED, my husband and I both went out to hunt the wild beast. We'd get up in the morning, grab our metaphorical clubs, put them in our real briefcases, and face our respective corporate jungles. We'd move through the underbrush of the week to the same rhythm. Together we hated Sunday night and groaned through Monday. We called each other from our desks, especially on a Monday morning after a vacation, and ask, "How bad is it? Are you awake yet?" Tuesday was better. Wednesday was "hump day," as in "getting over the hump and sliding into the weekend." Thursday was "the new Friday" and sometimes called for a dinner out to celebrate the almost-weekend. Friday was glorious and full of plans that usually didn't materialize before Sunday night moved in.

We both had good jobs and had worked since our teens, John in radio and government press offices, me on newspapers. We'd grown up focused, following our tracks through college like eager apprentices in trade school — broadcasting at Emerson College for John, journalism at Ohio State University for me. We graduated to do the work we loved, not caring about the clock, and not noticing that we weren't taking much time to play.

Somewhere in our forties, we looked back on our responsible youth and wished we'd blown a year being beach bums in Baja. Why hadn't we hitchhiked across Europe with the rest of America in the 1960s, or gone back to the land in Vermont, or run away to "find ourselves"? Because we'd never felt lost, I guess, and only started trying to jiggle the compass needle once we had a mortgage, aging parents, a vested pension plan, a 401k, and a middle-aged center of gravity that anchored us to a sensible path. Maybe the roots came from working too hard to grow them, or maybe it was just fear.

We'd fantasize about chucking it all for a cabin in the woods, about winning the lottery, or buying a B&B on the coast, a houseboat in the Keys, or a bright red convertible that we'd drive across the country with the top down and the radio blaring. I escaped vicariously by doing stories for the *Boston Globe* on the pressures of the rat race and how people dropped out of it, following their dreams to Alaska, to Maine, or to communes that still thrived in New England in the mid 1980s.

I took a class on running a bookstore and read a book on

how to become an innkeeper. I read *Do What You Love, The Money Will Follow* by Marsha Sinetar and wondered if I'd ever have the guts.

On Memorial Day, we'd imagine what it would be like to take the summer off. We'd say we'd take it for no money just to have the time. Oh, to have three months the way it used to be when they let us out of school until Labor Day! Three months to sit on the porch and read, drink lemonade, go to the beach, and be free, really free, to do everything or absolutely nothing.

Then it happened. A newspaper severance package dropped from the sky, and I got sprung. School let out forever and I was free, really free. But I was doing it alone, the kid who won the trip to Disneyland while her best friend stood outside the locked gate. John cheered the prize just as I would have cheered his. We both knew it was a good deal. We both knew I had to go. And we both knew Sunday night just got harder.

HE WATCHES ME PICK UP A BOOK at 10 p.m. and settle into a long read the way I used to only if Monday were a holiday. I see him feeling the weekend closing down, hanging a shirt on the closet door, giving up on the unread Sunday paper, checking the e-mail, making notes for a meeting, and setting the clock radio.

I've learned not to think out loud about which day would be better for a long lunch with old *Globe* pals, or if it might be fun to join a garden club. I try to keep some of the old workweek pace, setting my alarm a little earlier than his so I can get up and start the coffee, feed the cats, bring in the newspapers. I get ready for water aerobics as though it's a job. I am all efficiency packing the gym bag, filling the water bottle, tightening the lid on the thermal coffee mug. I'm going out there. Have to get to the pool by 8. In the rush hour. Work with weights. Exercise is hell.

I don't call him during the day to ask how it's going, especially on Monday after a vacation. We used to always wish for one more day, one more day. He doesn't need to hear from his partner, the human calendar, for whom the days now blend seamlessly into weeks, months, and years.

He doesn't need to live with the Energizer Bunny, who wants to say yes to dance lessons, a Great Books course, a poetry workshop, a spinning class, tai chi, an Elderhostel hike, and bird watching in the park at dawn. I try to remember the office metabolism, the exhaustion of a weekend hibernator, and what used to be my fervent prayer for all days off: *Phone, don't ring, and please, Lord, no social obligations.*

But I need to be social now, at least some of the time, and more often than before, I need to have him join me. So we work at meeting halfway between shutting down and firing up, reaching out our hands over the Disneyland gate. He tries ballroom dance, joins a cooking group, says yes to gatherings with friends even though he knows he'll be tired on that Friday or Saturday.

I have the dinner ready, put cut flowers in the living room, make sure fresh cloth napkins match the placemats, turn the radio to our favorite classical station, and ask, "How was your day?" He asks about mine.

We still play the fantasy game, asking: "If you could do anything at all right now, and didn't have to think about money, what would you do?" I tell him I'm doing it, having time to write. He says he's not sure what else he'd do right now.

We're living half a fantasy, and that has tilted the dream

toward practicality. We know he's too young to retire in his fifties. He's working for a regional chamber of commerce that values his talent. The economy has zapped our savings, and we need his salary.

The red convertible? Maybe we'll rent one for a couple weeks and see how far we get. Maybe I'll make a nice big picnic lunch with pork loin sandwiches and flat parsley.

Our fantasy-turned-half-real has given the marriage dance new steps. Our identities are not so easy to label: *working couple, reachable in the evenings, weekends sacrosanct.* I have days when I feel lost and self-conscious about drifting. He has days when he craves a vacation and would love to have my permanent one. But we're learning that down at the relationship bedrock, we are who we always were. And that's okay. Better than okay.

CHAPTER 11

"So, How's the Writing Going?"

That old nemesis, time, swinging in his hammock, watching me blow the day on pork loins, laundry, and feminist recalibrations, loves it when people ask this question. He especially loves it when they ask it with quizzical smiles the way they might inquire about a hobby, say an interest in growing bonsai or raising ferrets.

"Dilettante!" he snorts. "Tell them you haven't written a paragraph since last Thursday."

Nobody asked how the writing was going when I had a job. The going of the writing was fairly obvious because it went into the newspaper. People could get their hands dirty touching it and lining their birdcages with it. They could say, "I liked your piece this morning," or "What a crock of crap." Either way, there was a paycheck and an editor with another deadline demanding more.

Now there is neither. Now there is complete freedom and rejection slips, and it's easy to drown in both, particularly when The Writer has opened her trap and told friends, relatives, people on the street, anyone who asked, that she really wants to try fiction because she finally "has the time."

"Fiction, my Aunt Fanny," laughs the guy in the hammock, almost falling out of it.

My advice to anyone planning to write fiction in retirement is to say you're growing bonsai and raising ferrets. They're easier to explain, even if a few years have gone by and they haven't brought in a dime. Bonsai and ferrets can be explained with "I did it for love," which is believable when referring to the exquisite and the furry, but ludicrous when it's about a human being sitting alone at a computer keyboard all day, mostly hitting the delete key.

And those are the good days. So many of them can pass with The Writer getting nowhere near the delete key, let alone a plot, because there is much more pressing business to attend to, like:

the hornet in the kitchen,
the burned-out bulb in the ceiling light with the tricky cover
  that requires a balancing act on the sink,
the vet appointment for the cat,
the vet appointment for the other cat,
the oil change,
the last day of the sock sale,
reading the confusing medical bill,
reading an incorrect "notice of deficiency" from the IRS,
waiting on hold for the insurance company and the government,
the need for printer paper and a cartridge,
the e-mail from a high-school friend not heard from since
  1963.

And there is no deadline, which feeds all of the above and makes procrastination a virtue because important things are being accomplished, and there's no sense trying to squeeze writing into an hour here or 40 minutes there when I'll have Saturday. Is there?

That's when the words on a laminated sign above the home-office desk echo like the voice of God through a wasted brain: *"Nulla dies sine linea.* Never a day without a line — Horace 65–8 B.C." That was the motto of the late Don Murray, who wrote so perfectly about aging in his *Globe* column "Over 60," later named "Now and Then." He handed out the Latin placard to journalists at writing workshops he gave at the Poynter Institute in St. Petersburg and at newspapers around the country.

And he lived the words, for the author, Pulitzer Prize-winning editorial writer, and University of New Hampshire Professor Emeritus of English wrote every day until he died at age 82 in 2006. He insisted there was no such thing as writer's block. "Do plumbers skip work because they have plumber's block?" he'd say, noting that writing was a trade, a job like any other, and that the work gets done when the writer sits down and does it.

Next to the laminated sign is another quote from Don that I've printed in big red letters on an index card. "S.O.F.T.," it says, looking almost Shakespearian. I got it from Chip Scanlan, Poynter writing teacher, who told the crowd at Don's memorial service that his friend sent him the acronym for inspiration. "S.O.F.T." stands for "Say One Fuckin' Thing."

Inspire it does, and I say it out loud when I'm finally sitting down to do the work and wishing I'd been a plumber.

That blank screen and the freedom to write anything mirror a retiree's day, with its freedom to *do* anything. Both can be at once exhilarating and paralyzing. Anything? Will it be French lessons, pottery, volunteering, gardening, or just hanging out at home? If I hang out, should I wash the windows, clip the hedges, paint the fence, bicycle into the park because it's going to rain the rest of the week, or call friends?

If I write that short story, is the main character a detective, a newspaper reporter, a minister, an irritating neighbor, or a homeless man? Is the homeless man a former banker, teacher, mountain climber, or waiter? Is he fat or emaciated? Does he speak with a slight Eastern European accent? Why? Is his wife looking for him? No. His wife died in the fire. What fire? The one in the restaurant started by the mountain climber.

No, no, no. Write about what you know. I should write about my mother and my grandmother. But whose story is it? Mine? Theirs? My father's? Maybe it should be a play? No, a memoir. No, a poem. Has anybody seen my genre?

I am determined not to do journalism. No magazine pieces, op-ed columns, editorials, features. Nothing I've already done. I want no limits, no map, and no interview notes. I want whatever is lurking in the subconscious. Hello? I wait, often frozen, without facts. The process feels like constipation of the brain with all the possibilities seizing up and in need of literary prune juice.

I take two tablespoons at adult-education classes where teachers give assignments: write about someone saying good-bye to a house, write about an object, turn a dream into a story, eavesdrop on a conversation. I find more juice in books with writer prompts: write about a secret, write about the house of your childhood, write about someone you hate, someone you love. Exercises are supposed to coax words out from under their rocks and silence the inner editor who never likes anything except the delete key.

My friend Judith and I have challenged ourselves to pick a prompt, set a time, and write for 15 minutes a day, five days a week. On Friday we each choose one of our exercises and e-mail it. Our motto: Send It Even If It Sucks. (The Don Murray influence.) Working on longer pieces, I call her in Ithaca, read fragments on scraps of paper, and ask if they sound stupid. She assures me they don't and reads me her scraps.

I join a writing group that includes novelists, poets, and short-story and nonfiction writers, ages 30 to 70. They started meeting in 2006, gathering at the local Barnes & Noble every Wednesday night at 7:30. Anywhere from six to a dozen people show up. About half of them have been published, and all are dedicated to the masochistic, addictive, noble exercise of wrestling with words until they seem near perfect and are ready to be sent out for what will be almost certain rejection. Nobody should do that without a support group. Too many sharp objects on the desk.

Literary magazines can take six to eight months to respond to a piece. One man in the group didn't hear anything for two years, and when he finally got the rejection he couldn't remember writing the story.

He and other fiction veterans in the group send a story out to 10 or 15 magazines at once, ignoring the edict against simultaneous submissions, and when those come back they send out to 10 or 15 more. The more they send out, the greater the odds of selling. Simple mathematics, they say.

But a basic law of physics is at work here. Literary magazines are inundated and have only so many pages to fill, which means they can't use most of what comes in. This is the "two objects cannot occupy the same space" problem. Or maybe it's the "nature abhors a vacuum" thing. Either way, 10 pounds of literature will not fit in a five-pound bag.

And magazine editors seem to be glad this is so. Although some magazines are friendly and welcoming to the new writer, there is a whole lot of imperious going on.

"Our literary standards are as high as we can enforce them," one journal tells writers in its submission guidelines, sounding more like the state police. "We do not have the staff to engage in major editorial rewriting, except on rare occasions when the content justifies the effort."

Another journal tells writers to "please refrain from inquiring about a manuscript's status until at least five months have passed. We prefer that authors send a note with a self-addressed stamped envelope rather than contact us via phone or e-mail."

Writers are warned by a magazine that they must submit no more than two pieces during the eight-month reading period and that they may not send a second submission until hearing about the first. "We will cross-reference our databases periodically, and if we find more than one active submission, or a third submission (or more) during the reading period, all submissions will be immediately and summarily rejected unread."

So there.

The writing group explains that there is a hierarchy to rejections, and anything with handwriting on it means a piece was most likely considered by a senior editor. When I see "Thanks for sending us this story!" written across the bottom of a pro forma rejection card, I bring it in to the group for analysis. They say it should be interpreted as encouragement to send more. I do, and get another rejection with exactly the same note, including exclamation point, written across the bottom of the card.

Another rejection comes with indecipherable handwritten initials at the bottom of the standard "thanks but no thanks" letter and "best wishes" written on top. Should I get excited? Are the editors sending me a signal? And what does it mean when an editor writes, "I am truly sorry we can't use this story"? He's the editor, already. He doesn't have to be sorry. He can publish the damn thing and make us both truly happy.

A typed response from a magazine says the writing is "lively and interesting" and the editors enjoyed reading it but "it isn't right for us." They don't want lively and interesting? They're looking for half-dead and boring? The last line is typed in boldface: **This is not our customary rejection slip.**

I feel like a code cracker in the Defense Department, or one of those Soviet watchers who used to check out what was going on at Lenin's tomb to see what the Kremlin really meant. Are these rejections or are they almost-acceptances? And if they are almost-acceptances, should I welcome the returned manuscripts that keep landing in the mailbox like dead carrier pigeons because they mean I can try again and am surely getting close?

As a writer friend says when we meet over coffee, "You have to be insane to keep doing this."

She's got a point, and maybe I'm proving it when I peek through the slats of the venetian blinds at the mailman. I want to see if he's carrying a big brown envelope, which most likely will contain a rejected manuscript. Seeing it ahead of time and being able to prepare for a downer is better than finding it cold in the box. Don't ask me why.

Writers are strange folk, especially at the post office, where they mess with too much paper. First a self-addressed envelope has to be weighed and stamped with the manuscript inside it so that the postage will be correct when the publisher mails it back, presumably within the author's lifetime and before the price of stamps goes up. After being weighed, the manuscript is removed and placed inside a second envelope addressed to the publisher. The self-addressed stamped envelope is folded in half and stuffed in there, too, along with a cover letter. Then everything is weighed and stamped again as the line at the post office gets longer.

Some writers don't bother with return envelopes and just let their stories go into the recycling bin, the black hole of literary death, or wherever creative sweat expires. Others choose to make online submissions only so they have no paperwork and can get the bad news by pithy e-mail. I want the body back. I want closure.

On rainy days, I show up at the post office with my envelopes in plastic bags so the address ink won't get wet and smear. Fiddling with plastic and paper, I hear people in line coughing and shuffling their feet. I wonder if the postal clerk has kept track and knows this is the eighth submission of a short story, and if she wishes I'd buy a ferret. I wonder if the mailman has told her I'm a window peeper.

One day I make the mistake of using the word "manuscript" when asking the clerk to weigh it in the self-addressed envelope.

"There's a manuscript in here?" she asks, way too loudly, shaking the envelope. "It's so light."

"It's a short piece," I tell her just above a mumble, feeling the heat creep up my back. "A memoir, sort of an essay thing."

"When you said 'manuscript' I pictured something big," she says, peering inside.

"It's in there," I say, knowing I should stop talking but don't.

"Four pages. It was longer, but I cut it."

I can hear the people with passport applications sighing. A kid is starting to cry. I consider grabbing everything, bolting for the car, driving to another town, and starting over at a different counter. But I keep messing with envelopes and flaps and bags and small change. And then I go home to wait for the mailman.

I am one of thousands, maybe millions, who are waiting for the mailman. I am one of thousands, maybe millions, poring over the writer magazines and books, getting pitches for conferences, retreats, lectures, and supporting the business that sells the selling of words. The business sells way more than most of the buyers do or ever will. Is that a rip-off? Sometimes. But I get good advice as well as huckstering. I read good writing in the journals as well as pretentious junk. So I press on in this place that is no longer the press and keep typing, on good days, hoping that the writing will go better before it goes worse.

I'm living a fantasy that began as a kid when I watched my father working his short-story writing around his job as an insurance salesman. He sold the pieces to outdoor and mystery magazines. His old Underwood sits on the bookcase in my bedroom office. I look at it from the computer chair and remember pounding out bad mysteries and horse and dog stories for junior high English classes. The shift key clanked and shook the wobbly typewriter table, which banged against the pine board wall of our drafty basement recreation room in Cleveland. The keys slapped hard on the paper, often jamming, and my fingers turned black separating the letters. The noise and the ink made me feel like a famous writer. I typed as hard as I could, rang the bell, sent the carriage flying, and imagined growing up to be Carolyn Keene, Albert Payson Terhune, or Marguerite Henry.

The keyboards got quieter and more sophisticated over the years — Royal portable, Smith Corona electric, Epson, Gateway, Hewlett-Packard. The day job at the newspaper took my energy, and there was never enough time to do the assignments for night classes in short-story or play writing. But the fiction fantasy remained pretty much the same naïve little bundle of nerve endings that it was at age 14. The difference is that now people are more interesting than horses, dogs, and teenage sleuths, and I want to grow up to be Nora Ephron, Joan Didion, or Neil Simon. Also, the fantasy has never run into so much reality.

"Don't you miss being published?" people ask.

"Naaaaaa," I tell them. "Been there, done that. Obscurity is swell."

Was it time to try *The Rejected Quarterly*? That's the magazine "featuring fine literature rejected at least five times."

"First in the field of rejection since 1998," the editors say on the Web site. "We offer quality offbeat fiction you can't find anywhere else." Writers must submit five rejection slips from other journals when sending to *TRQ*. "No other literary journal maintains such strict standards," the editor boasts.

I make copies of five rejections, assure the editors in a cover letter that I can provide more, and go to the post office feeling like a bigger dweeb than usual. I keep the envelope with the journal's name hidden while waiting in line and hope a clerk doesn't read it out loud. I sweat the weighing of the envelopes, shove the stationery around, and finally get the packet off to the California editorial office, which promises to respond in "one to six months."

In three months, I see the journal's e-mail address in the computer inbox and feel a tiny current of hope. I tamp it down, figuring the inevitable must be coming electronically. I close my eyes and click the mouse, open them a slit and read:

"Hi Susan. This is Dan Weiss of *The Rejected Quarterly*. We enjoyed your story, 'Branding,' and would like to use it in the upcoming issue."

I read that five or 10 times. I print it out and read it again. I yell "YeeeeeHaaaaa!" in the silent house and try to fist bump with the cats. I e-mail everybody in the writing group. I hug my father's Underwood.

It doesn't matter that most people have never heard of *The Rejected Quarterly* or that the publication will look mighty strange listed on my resume. It doesn't matter that I've spent more than two years sending the short story around to nine magazines, or that payment is a free copy and $15, which barely covers postage and envelopes. All I feel in the heat of a literary lightning strike on this glorious Friday afternoon in July is crazy, wild, cockeyed joy.

→ CHAPTER 12 ←

It's Just the Wind

What was that?

Nothing.

Scared the hell out of me.

You tripped. No big deal.

Tripped over what? My feet? Bam! All of a sudden I'm down on the pavement in the park on a summer day on level ground looking like a fool.

It's a skinned knee. Relax.

And a swollen ankle.

No broken bones. No sprains. Ice it and shut up.

That's not the point.

There's a point here?

Stop being dismissive.

That's my job. I'm the left brain. I dismiss nonsense.

You don't care that I looked like a fool?

You don't care that you sound like one?

I'm flat out on the ground and this old guy in an SUV pulls

up and says, "Are you all right, dear?" like it would never happen to him and like he's looking around for my walker, or maybe a gurney.

Forget it.

Can't.

Try.

It happened on the street once, too. Last year, remember? I'm walking sideways, looking up at a tree, and sort of tip over.

Don't walk sideways.

They say the balance starts to go as you get older.

They?

Doctors. Scientists. People.

Never mind the almighty They. Just watch where you're going.

Did I lose focus? Did the mind wander off?

For a second or two, maybe.

That's all it takes, a second or two.

It?

An accident. A broken hip.

Didn't happen.

I don't remember falling when I worked.

That's because you spent most of the day in a car or in a chair.

I get scared sometimes now.

And talk to yourself.

A little.

A lot.

You don't have to answer.

Left brain talks logic to right.

This has nothing to do with logic.

You're telling me?

Things happen to people is all I'm saying, and I think about that more than I did when I was too busy to think about it.

You're fine.

This is bigger than the damn ankle, okay? It's about the whole world, the universe, everything I love.

John is fine.

That week in the hospital?

He had a staph infection. He took care of it.

Out of nowhere on a Saturday night he gets the chills so bad the whole couch is shaking. In 90 minutes his fever is 103. What if we'd been away, camping or hiking, miles from a doctor?

You weren't.

No cuts. No broken skin. But somehow the thing attacks. Bam! His leg turns bright red like a terrible sunburn and he can't touch it.

Germs. They're everywhere. Sometimes they get in. Antibiotics get them out.

Not if they're super germs. Then they kill you.

He didn't have super germs.

But he could have.

Get a grip.

He's in the hospital bed in the same wing where his mother was dying the year before. He's got an IV hooked up. I'd never seen him in a hospital bed. He'd never seen me in one. We've hardly seen each other sick.

You're lucky.

I know. But it gets you thinking.

Catastrophizing.

The hospital takes over your life. It's all loud announcements and lights and people coming in to take blood or to bring pills in little cups, except when you really need them. And there's a guy in the next bed groaning because his back is killing him. It's surreal, out of control, when just the day before everything was quiet and normal.

Roll with it.

A friend wakes up at 6 A.M. and takes her husband to the hospital because his pulse is racing at double time. Something called supraventricular tachycardia. Short circuit in the electronics of the heart.

Very common. Not dangerous.

Another friend has quintuple bypass surgery. Somebody else goes in for prostate surgery.

All recovered. All doing fine. Fine, fine, fine.

But until you know that, and even after you do, the memory of it still feels an awful lot like fear, like that noise in the dark when you were a kid, like the bogeyman.

No such thing as the bogeyman.

A woman I used to work with has Alzheimer's. She was like a big sister. That's the bogeyman.

That's disease.

A friend's sister dies in her sleep just after her 60th birthday. Another friend, who's had cancer, sits across the lunch table and says in a matter-of-fact voice, like she's talking about the soup, "I don't know if I've got another 20 years."

She could easily have 30.

Yes, but . . .

So don't obsess. She's not.

John says maybe we shouldn't get kittens when our old cats

go because that could be a 20-year commitment, and who knows if we can do animals in our eighties.

Nobody knows. Might as well get the kittens.

It's not that simple.

Why?

I read the obituary pages.

Switch to the comics.

I read both.

Then you should have perspective.

Susan Butcher, the dogsled champion, died of leukemia at age 51. I interviewed her in Alaska, rode with her through the woods, sat in her cabin. She was strong, beautiful, solid, permanent. She won the Iditarod race four times. Anchorage to Nome, 1,150 miles.

Remember the strength.

Something moves in. Bam! And they're gone.

Remember perspective.

Too many familiar faces in the obits.

Don't look. You hardly glanced at the obits when you were at the paper.

Didn't have to. Everybody was young and healthy and down the hall.

Mortality happens. It is the natural order.

That's what my doctor says.

Speaking generally, not specifically.

But she's looking at me when she says, "Something eventually gets all of us."

That's true. It does.

Not what you want to hear from your medical professional.

She's being philosophical, telling you not to sweat what you can't control.

No control. That's why I shiver sometimes.

Put on a sweater.

Maybe I need to feel the fear. In the quiet, in my head, just between us, right brain and left.

Wouldn't you rather work on a crossword puzzle?

I have to stop being busy and listen.

To what? To me?

To all of it. To the noise in the dark, to the wind.

It's better to keep moving.

I don't like to drive at night now. I cancel dinners when it snows. I used to drive in anything.

Keep moving in the daytime in clear weather.

There are new pills on the dresser. Blood-pressure medication, eye drops. It used to be just multiple vitamins.

All controllable conditions. Follow the instructions on the label.

It's more than that.

No it's not.

You don't feel vulnerable?

I do but I can deal.

So can I.

Then why are we having this discussion?

Because I thought I heard something, felt something, lost something.

You tripped in the park.

And it felt like a metaphor for the whole cosmic megillah.

I don't do metaphors.

I needed to talk about it.

Don't talk so much. Just live.

Like a tightrope walker, dancing beautifully with the umbrella and not looking down.

It's best that way, dancing beautifully.

It's terrifying.

Yes.

CHAPTER 13

Stuff

The plan is to unload, to simplify. The plan is to clear surfaces, clean out corners, and become the photo in the newspaper ad with the headline: "Imagine your home totally organized!"

"Gonna rent a dumpster and get at it," I'd say when I worked and the concept was so easy to relegate to some future weekend, to next spring, or next fall. "Gonna call that guy with his number on the telephone pole: *1-800-Got Junk?*"

"All I need is time," I'd say as the walls of the garage moved in on the cars, the boxes in the attic pushed to the edge of the hole that opens up around the pull-down stairway in the hall ceiling, and the things that go bump in the shadows of the oil burner seemed to whisper, "She doesn't have a clue what's in here."

I would haul them out, name them, and send them away so no one else would have to. So the nieces, nephew, and second cousins wouldn't stand there the way John and I stood in his mother's basement, the way my brother, Dan, and I stood in our mother's garage, and the way my mother stood in her mother's living room, gaping at the tonnage and groaning the question nearly every generation asks of the one previous: "What are we supposed to do with all this crap?"

We found a grenade in my mother's garage, probably a souvenir from my dad's World War II army tour in the Aleutian Islands. The pin was in it, and nobody wanted to pull it out. We called the Orlando police, who sent over people from the bomb squad. If I remember correctly, they dropped it in a bucket of water and determined it was a dud. The crowd that had gathered on the street outside the police tape was disappointed.

We found two pistols in my mother-in-law's basement when we were moving her to an apartment near us. They had belonged to her father, who was chief of police in Derby, Connecticut. My husband took them down to the station, hoping he wouldn't be stopped on the way for some traffic violation and asked to explain why he was packing heat.

My mother found collections of heavy vases and figurines at my grandmother's house and probably felt like using them as weapons as she set them out on tables for a yard sale. Grandma was also being moved from a house into an apartment but had no clear sense of diminishing dimensions. She kept taking items back into the house and removing the tags. Sometimes she snatched things out of people's hands and told them to keep their money.

Before I go that dotty, before the grenade rolls out of the oil-burner room — unless it's at Dan's house — before the relatives shake their heads at crazy old Aunt Sue hanging on to a 1970s three-speed bicycle with flat tires, I would break free of the tyranny of things.

Except that I haven't.

Okay, I've given away nine pairs of shoes that killed my feet. That was easy. I've taken a carload of old office power-suits to the Goodwill. That was a relief. I've thrown out corroded salt and pepper shakers, dead Christmas lights, and shredding towels — all of which would have made a barely audible thump in a dumpster, had a dumpster been rented, which it wasn't.

That's because the big stuff that I planned to "get at" is mostly getting at me. The truth about simplifying is what truth often turns out to be on closer inspection under the bare bulb of reality: complicated.

I reach into the cobwebs for the furnace-room whisperers and find love. There in the corners is John's pre-Digital Age photo equipment — developing trays, printing papers, drying clips, darkroom safe lights, film canisters, enlarger, filters, light meters, and a lot of other relics surpassed by technology. We both have digital cameras. John has Photoshop on his computer. We need this stuff like Henry Ford needed a horse.

But I could no more pitch this pile of antiques than give away the wedding album. For eight years, John ran a freelance photo business out of the basement. He left a good-paying job to do it and made exactly the right move for his soul. These were years of happy sweat and long hours, taking courses in Boston, New York, and Maine, learning on assignment for area newspapers and businesses, and scrambling up a trail that took him from amateur to pro — and ultimately to his next full-time job.

I look at the pile and hear the ceiling fan running in the old, tiny bathroom, smell the chemicals, feel the wind blowing through the open back door on a late January night, and see portraits swimming to life in trays on the workbench. I see John, energized and young, watching the trays, waiting for the exhilaration that can never quite be duplicated by the click of a mouse. Photography the way it used to be. Us the way we used to be. The reasons we named our cats "Ansel" for Adams and "Berenice," with three e's, for Abbott.

The whisperers go back into their corners.

The broken toy gorilla in the back of the guestroom closet is so encased in dust it looks white. I'd forgotten it was there. It was a gag gift that made me laugh at a time when I was crying a lot, trying to change jobs. Before the motion-detector mechanism died, the gorilla would jump up and down, rattle the bars of the cage, and shout, "Help! Please! Somebody get me out of here!" whenever anyone walked past. It still makes me laugh, and it's still sitting in the dust next to the vacuum cleaner.

The three-speed bicycle leaning against paint cans and extra bird feeders in the garage would work fine with new tires. I bought it in Quincy, Massachusetts, when everything with wheels was easier to understand. I would need a consultant to make this purchase today. (They want to sell me *how* many gears?) I would need training, funny shorts, and maybe a neck brace to keep the head up while hunched over the curling handlebars. Would this be simplifying? Is trading up the way to pare down? Would it be like the time John and I tried to replace our old, two-slot toaster and came home with a countertop oven the size of a Volkswagen?

I'll think about the bike later, along with deferred decisions about hoses, wood scraps, bags of potting soil, saws, sawhorses, and fluorescent lamps that don't quite fit anywhere, but that somebody might want someday, maybe.

Possible future utility explains a lot in the garage. The fold-up banquet table that hasn't been unfolded since a Thanksgiving in the 1980s, the hedge clippers in all sizes — electric and manual — the snow shovel collection, from light-weight collapsible to back-breaker, the duplicate garden tools resting against the garden tool holder, still in its box and waiting for a clear wall so it might be installed. We know young people who will buy a house one day and may want some of this stuff. We can be useful. That's important now, being useful — maybe more important than being neat.

Legacy is important now. When my mother-in-law, Alice, died, John and I graduated to oldest generation in his family. We felt the full weight of being Keepers of the Flame and Archives, especially while lugging home boxes of Alice's beloved Waterford crystal. I'd felt that kind of responsibility less when my mother died because most of the heavy stuff went home with my brother, who had three kids, a bigger house, and a U-Haul trailer. But John is an only child, and there's no dumping Great Aunt May.

She's also in the garage. The giant, heavy, red-framed photograph of John's grandmother's sister, taken in the early 1880s when she was around age 3, sits in a box on a shelf under our luggage. Alice kept her under the bed in the apartment. The portrait was way too big for the walls, and nobody else wanted her. Alice didn't want her either but could never have disowned the little girl who became the fearsome matriarch, no matter how unpleasant the memories. Great Aunt May was, is, and will always be family.

So is Great Uncle Charles, May's brother. He's in the laundry room. His much smaller photograph, taken when he was an adult looking a little like Jackie Gleason, fits nicely in a wicker basket next to the clothes dryer. He shares the basket with one of John's father's campaign posters from an election for town clerk and a photograph of a skinny guy with a mustache. I'm not too sure who the skinny guy is but can't toss him either.

People do dump their relatives at flea markets like so much trash, leaving them to stare blankly from musty corners of barns on Route 1 in Maine, or to peer up out of shoe boxes loaded with postcards selling for five cents apiece. These abandoned faces are surrounded by Coca-Cola trays, jelly jars, rotary-dial telephones, dry sinks, Howdy Doody puppets, and toasters like our old one, built before bagels. The faces always look as though they want to go home, even though home is now a generation they wouldn't know, living in a century they wouldn't understand.

Our attic is full of people who are "home," most of them inherited from my mother and grandparents, most of them unframed, undated, and unidentified. Part of the preretirement fantasy was that I'd put the familiar faces into archival-quality albums with brief histories so the nieces, nephew, and second cousins would know their relatives. But this has not happened, perhaps because of a genetic defect inherited from parents and grandparents who didn't bother with such details either.

And there are so many unfamiliar faces, often standing with their arms around the people I know, or bobbing up out of what may or may not be Lake Michigan in bathing suits that look like long undershirts. There are immense group shots at picnics with women in long dresses and men in straw hats looking at the photographer who must be saying, "Okay, everybody squeeze in tight, all 50 of you." The features are so tiny they can hardly be seen with a magnifying glass. The occasions are long forgotten. But these people are ours. Boxes of them.

The Polish Christmas ornaments handed down from great

grandmothers are up there. My father's short stories are up there in a box with his army hat and medals, along with my Great Uncle Martin's sheet music and singing reviews, along with my mother's stage pictures from New York, where she never became famous but lived her dreams. The old *Boston Globe* newspaper clippings are up there too, by the ton. The *Globe* has them all on file. But those are electronic and theirs. These are yellow, disintegrating, and mine.

Can I toss the tarnished pair of belly-dancer finger cymbals? I remember my mother on the phone announcing she'd signed up for a belly-dancing class. She was in her sixties then, which seemed old, but seems young now. We found them in her dresser drawer when we cleaned out her house. And someone will find them in mine.

Can I toss the little homemade embroidered bag with the fake pearl sweater clip that I gave her once for Mother's Day? There's a hand-carved willow whistle in the bag, too, that Grandpa made for Grandma when they were courting. There are two hospital baby identification bracelets, my brother's and mine, and my mother's engagement and wedding rings.

I pick through stuff not worn in decades: a charm bracelet, a topaz ring that was a confirmation present, the cultured pearl pin my piano teacher gave me for high school graduation, old watches, and a 45-year-old purse mirror from the Hilltop Beauty Salon, where my mother got her hair done in North Royalton, Ohio. I re-open the boxes containing pins, earrings, and bracelet presents from friends. I take everything out and put it all back.

I'm just as bad with the mundane daily detritus that grows on the kitchen counter, the coffee tables, and the desks. It doesn't carry the same emotional freight but makes its demands as unrelentingly as Great Aunt May. Unread copies of the *New Yorker* and *National Geographic*, in-depth newspaper articles on the Middle East and long-term-care insurance that will be gone over thoroughly one day "when I have time," unread books, and a *Real Simple* magazine featuring 99 ideas for "whipping your space into shape." Why are magazines that specialize in simplification always so fat?

Directions for appliances, warranties, recall notices, and service contracts pile up in the kitchen, along with coupons for freebies and "important changes in the terms of your charge account," never mind that I haven't read the original.

"Dear Sir or Madam," begins a letter from a shareholder services company I didn't know I was involved with. "While we have no reason to believe your information has been or will be accessed or misused, we are writing to inform you of an incident involving personal information that we maintain. On February 27, 2008, our archive services vendor notified us that they could not account for one of several boxes of data backup tapes that they were transporting to an off-site storage facility. The missing tapes contained personal account information."

The letter goes on, and on, crafted by a committee of attorneys, who bounce back and forth between assurance and the need for vigilance. I decide to be assured, but vigilantly save the letter, and will, no doubt, save it for years. The nieces, nephew, and second cousins will probably discover it in the file with the will.

I have theatre and concert programs that go back to the 1980s. I have half-dead plants, or half-alive plants as a more positive take would put it. I've got piles of CDs that don't fit in the wobbly CD tower and are making their own towers all over the house. I have recipes lying around with newsletters about organic eggs that came in the carton with the eggs. I have printouts of e-mails from friends, placed on the table so I won't forget to answer them. An identical e-mail from several people is headed: "VERY IMPORTANT! BIG VIRUS COMING!!! READ AND FORWARD. DO NOT DELETE." I don't. Oh, how I do not delete.

"YOU NEED TO DE-CLUTTER," the in-home design consultant from the furniture store says, looking around the living room where every flat surface is nicked, dented, or covered with stuff. In addition to our sagging 20-year-old couches, we have squeezed in Alice's overstuffed chair and footstool, her rocking chair, dining-room buffet, and china cupboard. We also have her surly 16-year-old cat.

Professional help seems like a good idea. We will focus on just this one room and then try to move on to the gorilla. We watch the brisk woman measuring, pacing, shaking her head, and talking to herself. She hates the rug but will work with it.

"What else do you want to keep?" she asks.

John and I have agreed to go cold turkey in this room and tell her everything is expendable except maybe the china cupboard. We see her frown. "But, you know, if it has to go," I stammer.

"I'll work with it," she says.

"Great," John says, sounding more confident than he feels. "You come up with a plan, and we'll take care of the rest."

Yeah, right. Us and whose army?

The process takes months, involving painters, a carpenter, the hauling of old furniture to a charity for the homeless, the purging of three bookcases, none of which look purged after 25 boxes of books go to the Hingham library. We discover we have merely made room for the volumes that had been wedged sideways on the tops of other volumes or stacked on the floor.

We move it all downstairs to replace the older and even more densely packed bookcases that we plan to clear out and give away. We don't. We move the older ones into the laundry room with Great Uncle Charlie, John's father, and the skinny guy. All the bookcases remain loaded.

But the living room could make the pages of *Real Simple*. It's a stunner with the wall unit holding the TV, stereo, and every single CD, alphabetized. The mantle looks like a still life, holding nothing but a clock and a reproduction of an antique mug. Only a few judiciously placed photos of the young people decorate the bookshelves, along with a couple carefully stacked clusters of books.

"We have a grown-up living room," John says sitting carefully in the striped swivel chair, color coordinated to match the brown couch and walls. "Does that mean we're grown-ups?"

No. It means we can't let company go downstairs or, God forbid, into the attic. It means the surly cat won't go into the living room anymore because he thinks he's in the wrong house. And sometimes we think we are, too.

It will get messy again. I know this for sure three years into retirement. I know that clutter will make inroads into the perfect room faster than any plans to organize will move outward. Clutter is where we live, and this business of sorting through a house in one's sixties is not so much about having time as it is about having roots. Maybe Grandma wasn't so dotty after all.

→ CHAPTER 14 ←

Unfinished Business

S orting through old photos and mementoes, I kick up ghosts as well as dust. Some flit past like butterflies, lovely little memories that bring smiles. Some are more like sentries, standing tall, protective, and proud of their child, their friend, their connection with the past, unwavering in their encouragement and love.

But others clutch sharply at a sleeve and stare, their eyes a mix of accusation and sadness. I stare back, remembering, caught, wishing I could make things right. Is that what they want — the wish, the acknowledgment, the perspective to see them clearly? I try but cannot put them to rest. Is *that* what they want?

CEIL STANDS IN THE DOORWAY of her tiny one-floor brick house built across the street from our white, wooden, two-story. She is about to come out to work on her flowers, but she stops, listening, waiting.

"God dammit, Ceil. Where the hell are you?" Her husband,

Jim, is exploding somewhere in the house, his voice so loud he could be standing on our porch.

"You did WHAT?" he shouts at his two little girls. "Answer me. Answer me right now." Jim is a big man with wheezy breath and a red face, and his temper is legend. Ceil is tall, too thin, and her delicate, slightly trembling fingers play around her lips when she talks.

My mother sometimes stops to chat about weather or meat prices on the way to the store if Ceil is in the front yard watering the garden. My father and Jim wave and chat if they're both out washing their cars. They talk Nash Ramblers and Fords.

Jim's temper is a kind of joke to my parents. "There goes Jim," my father says as we eat dinner at the squeaky yellow Formica table in our cramped kitchen. "He's loud, but he's a good guy. Nicest guy in the world to talk to."

"She understands him," my mother says of Ceil. "Just quietly takes it all in and calms him down." As a kid I accept yelling fathers as a way of life, even though mine is quiet. Yelling is a right of patriarchy in post–World War II Cleveland. Fathers have jobs and stress.

Maybe Jim was a good man. Maybe she did understand him and calm him down. Maybe they're still married. Or maybe we were all blind to what today would be an obvious abuser, at least verbally if not physically. Fifty-plus years later, I think of this woman surrounded by neat lawns in a middle-class neighborhood in a world where nobody talked about their marriages to Oprah or to anybody else.

I look at the photos of San Diego Avenue and see her, large eyes wide, quick hands touching her lips. Was she afraid of what might come tumbling out or was she trying to get up the nerve to speak of more than weather and meat prices?

Ceil, were you okay? Are you okay?

I SEE MISS SUBERT IN THE sixth-grade classroom, slapping her pointer stick against her palm. "Thirty seconds," she warns. As usual I am the last one standing at the blackboard. Eight or ten of us had been up doing long-division problems, but everybody else worked faster, chalk squeaking, white dust flying. I'm frozen, not seeing the numbers, hypnotized by the beat of the pointer stick, the wall-clock pendulum, and the sound of Miss Subert's high heels on the dirty wood floor as she comes closer.

A few people giggle. My chalk is wet with sweat. My armpits itch. My eyes sting. I can't swallow. Miss Subert is next to me now, an enormous woman with black hair, casting a shadow across my face. I hear her breathing, smell her talcum, jump as she smacks the pointer stick hard against the chalk tray. "You're not even trying, are you?" she snaps. "Erase and sit down."

Looking at the Garfield School class photo from 1957, I still want retribution. I want to go back, pointer stick in hand, to goose Miss Subert right out of that dark brick building, down the cement walk under the elm trees, and into the twenty-first century to face an angry jury of my peers. I want her to take the stand without the benefit of an attorney as I read the indictment.

You're the reason I hate numbers. You're the reason I cheated on math tests, copying answers from the girl next to me. You're the reason I go ballistic with bureaucratic rules and petty authority. You're the reason I started writing.

"I did like your essays, and you were a star in the reading group."

It was where I made up for being class fool. I read extra books and wrote extra reports to get approval. How healthy was that?

"You needed to be pushed in math."

Over a cliff?

"It wasn't that bad."

You stripped me bare under a spotlight — the long-division game, the timed-bell work problems, the homework that you made us do in ink with nothing crossed out, which was impossible.

"I was getting you ready for junior high school."

Nobody made us do math problems in ink in junior high.

"So it was a good exercise. It made what came next seem easy."

Parents today would sue your high heels off. The Montessori people would put you in jail. The whole school would be shut down for rigid, narrow-minded thinking. Your class was the capper on six years of tyrannical teachers hissing, "Shhhhhh! There will be no talking to our neighbors." They valued silence more than enthusiasm. More than anything else, they valued control. If I were in sixth grade today, I'd have tutors, psychologists, nurturing, understanding, and freedom.

"Life's a bastard, Missy. And the sooner a child learns that the better."

I learned to be scared, angry, and a cheat.

"And you're stronger for it now."

How do you know?

"Experience."

You had no right to be that mean.

"Tough love. It's made a comeback, I'm told."

In reform schools.

"You were overly sensitive. Too many Saturday morning Westerns. You saw the world as heroes or villains."

You thought you were both.

"I was doing my job the best way I knew how."

I want a better answer. I want an apology.

"You won't get one."

Thirty seconds.

"Oh, come now."

You're not even trying.

"That's your job."

UNCLE MARTIN POUNDS THE PIANO, filling the house with chords and his huge tenor voice. He sings in Italian, in German. It is beautiful — now.

"You thought it was noise back then," he says, looking up from the keys, laughing. The laugh is as big as his music, but his eyes are sad. "Opera was fat people howling gibberish. You'd say, 'He's not going to sing, is he?' You and your father thought I was a joke."

I hold a torn shoe box full of dusty, damaged cassette tapes. They're all that remain of his voice. He made them in his eighties, singing into a cheap tape recorder on his out-of-tune piano in a Florida trailer park. When I play them I can hear a tiny echo of the lung power people used to compare to Mario Lanza. Today they would say Pavarotti.

I'm sorry.

He doesn't hear me. He sings louder as I see family and friends gathered for one of his concerts in his living room. It is his treat, along with a meticulously prepared meal. I should know this is wonderful, but I'm focused on operatic caricature, on the flamboyant artiste who enters rooms hitting high notes, who boards the same city bus I take home from junior high school and serenades me while standing behind the driver's seat. All the passengers clap as I turn red, too self-conscious about not blending in with everyone else to appreciate the complex gift of this magnificent personality.

My father imitates him as we drive over to my uncle's crazy, multi-level house built into a hill overlooking Cleveland's Metropolitan Park. The house is full of stairways leading to bedrooms, balconies, bathrooms, closets. It looks like an Escher drawing that a strong wind might knock into the valley below. My dad winks at me in the rearview mirror and sings bastardized *Carmen*: "Toreador! Don't spit on the floor. Use the cuspidor. That's what it's for." My mother tells him to knock it off. He doesn't.

He nudges me and winks again in Uncle Martin's living room between concert pieces. We are both thinking of "The Toreador Song" and my sides hurt from trying not to laugh. My mother's thin fingers are tight on my arm. "That," she says in her steel voice, "is enough." There will be hell to pay in the car on the way home.

She loves opera because of Uncle Martin. He is her mother's brother, and she has been listening to him sing since she was a kid. She remembers how the neighbors would come out on the street to hear him practicing, even if he was just practicing scales.

Uncle Martin is the phenom in a family of good but not great singers. He has grown up a star of church choirs, amateur opera productions, and recital halls. He does local television shows in Cleveland and performs in nightclubs dressed as a Gypsy troubadour, ribbons streaming from his guitar. He catches the ear of Metropolitan Opera star Rosa Ponselle, who invites him to meet with her to discuss his career and the possibility of a scholarship to Juilliard. But she is late for the appointment, and

Uncle Martin goes into one of his snits, walking out on what would, most likely, have been international fame. He tosses off the blown connection as a waste of time. He doesn't need school. He knows how to sing.

The incident comes up at many holiday dinners. "How could you walk out, Martin?" He ends the questioning by standing up and hitting high notes, holding them until they overpower anybody who is talking.

There are no more big career breaks. He remains stubbornly small-time, slowly losing his voice to nightclub cigarette smoke and the lack of proper training. He supports himself as a floral arranger and night watchman for Halle's Department Store, loving the job because the store sells pianos and he can play them and sing long and loud into the night.

I can see him in the empty store, composing and writing poetry, which he sends to me in college and at the *Boston Globe*, and which I toss out. When I live in New York, he asks me to look up music publishers where he might send some of his compositions. I hear my father singing one of Uncle Martin's favorites in falsetto: "Swinging on the grapevine swing. Laughing where the wild birds sing." I don't look up the publishers.

He retires to his trailer in Florida and calls it heaven because it has a patio and a shade tree. He sends me pictures of himself feeding seagulls. He has a portrait done in a captain's hat and jacket with gold buttons. He says he is happier than he has ever been in his life.

He is in love. His lover is a man. They have always been men — something that should have been as obvious as his talent, but I missed that too until reading his diaries after he died.

"Your uncle is a fruit," my father would say when Martin was alive. He'd infuriate my mother by making a limp wrist motion. She'd tell him he didn't understand artists, or great music. She'd say Uncle Martin was a "confirmed bachelor," who only had time for his songs.

My dad, despite his instinctive reaction, was just as ignorant. He'd say of Henry, Uncle Martin's partner for more than 20 years, "Now, that guy is okay. Nothing wrong with Henry." We all adored Henry for his quiet intelligence, patient acquiescence to children who demanded that he play checkers as soon as he walked in the door, and for his ability to make Uncle Martin laugh.

But they split up after decades together. I'm not sure why. Maybe Henry needed quiet. Uncle Martin introduced us to other men friends. He traveled with them, talked about the arts with them, invited them to Florida. When he'd mention that one or the other had died, I'd say I was sorry but had no sense of what was lost.

Reading his diaries at the kitchen table in the trailer, I know. My mother and I are cleaning the place out in the spring of 1984. It is full of dead cockroaches, unpaid bills, and poetry scrawled on the backs of envelopes. The floor sags, and the piano, damaged by mold, is listing to one side.

In the diaries he writes about losing his lover the previous year, about the loneliness, about wanting him back and knowing there will never be anyone like him in his life again. Human grief has been the same since the first tear. Anyone alive knows what it is, and knows it demands consolation, especially from family. But I sit there, not having sent so much as a sympathy card, having no clear recollection of the man.

I'm sorry.

People who live in the trailer park come to the door to offer their condolences. They remember the poems he wrote for people's birthdays, the cards he made, the paintings, the concerts he'd give in the evening. And, yes, they came out to sit around his trailer and listen.

Letters come to my mother from around the country — men and women Uncle Martin visited in his travels, people delighted by his energy and love of life, people who heard him sing, people who miss him and say how lucky his family is to have had this magnificent soul.

I'm sorry.

He can't hear me. He's hitting high notes.

THE PIN IN MY JEWELRY BOX is nearly 50 years old. That's a cold fact, and I hold it in my hand, feeling its weight.

Sherry isn't yet half that age when she sends it to me as a high school graduation present in the summer of 1963. She isn't yet half that age when she commits suicide somewhere in Michigan. I can't remember what city, or if I ever knew it. I can't remember if it's 1965 or 1966 when I meet Dolores in a McDonald's and she says, "Sherry is no longer living." Dolores doesn't want to say "dead."

I had asked about Sherry the way people ask mutual friends what news they've heard, expecting the normal business of life, expecting to catch up. Couldn't you always catch up?

Dolores has few details, and nobody else in our high school class has them either. We have broken apart as classes usually do, heading for different colleges, different lives. Dolores knows only that Sherry killed herself after her boyfriend committed suicide.

I hadn't received a letter from Sherry for maybe a year. I

hadn't written one either. I don't know who stopped writing first, or if it matters. I could have written again. I could have called, although ours was a letter-writing generation. I could have tried harder not to lose her, unless maybe she wanted to be lost. But I don't know that either. I don't know anything. The only fact is the pin in my hand.

Why?

The tiny, quick high school girl recedes into the shadows. She cannot tell me. No one can tell me.

If I'd called you, if I'd gone to Michigan. . . .

"Fix your hair like this," the quick girl says, moving the part, poufing up the middle. She says I need tweaking rather than a complete overhaul. This is a relief because I'm the new kid at the school in this spring of 1962, a nervous junior year transplant to the suburbs from Cleveland's West Side. My grandfather has retired and moved in with us, so we need a bigger house. The move makes sense on paper, and the town is lovely, but the transition is ugly. I feel like a blob in a culture where skirts are shorter, haircuts are sharper, kissing happens faster, and the faces I'd known since kindergarten fade into a past life.

Sherry adopts me. She understands the stress at home, the moving boxes in the living room, the squabbling parents, a mother looking for a job when mothers didn't do that, an old man growing senile and fraying nerves. She understands my fear of taking driver's ed. with the cool kids.

We cry listening to her album of *West Side Story*. Oh, Bernardo! Oh, Tony! Sherry, Dolores, and I act out all the parts. We confess our crushes to each other, lamenting that the boys who are interesting and edgy ignore us, but the boring nice ones call.

"Run!" Sherry whispers and yanks me into the music department storeroom, where we climb into bass violin cases and pull the lids shut. We are dodging a boring nice boy we see coming down the hall. We've heard he wants to ask one of us out. We blow our cover by laughing so hard we rock the cases. The boy opens the lids and stares at us. He does not ask either of us out. *Remember, Sherry? You were so funny. So alive and—*

She shakes her head and closes her eyes, holding a finger to her lips.

It is fall of our senior year when Sherry announces that her family is moving from Ohio to Michigan. The news hits like one of those fierce fast storms that blow in off Lake Erie. Her father is changing jobs, making another one of those moves that look good on paper, being responsible in that unfathomable adult way. The decision seems heartless to Sherry, Dolores, and me. He couldn't wait until June? He couldn't let her graduate with us?

Is that when it started? The depression? You never said. You were so up.

She waves a fistful of letters, smiling. We write volumes to each other after she moves, detailing who is breaking up, who is going out, the latest parental outrages, what books we are devouring, what music moves us, what movie stars we'd like to marry. How I love seeing her return address in the mail pile on the kitchen shelf. I save the letter for after dinner, after homework, to read slowly. Sometimes I answer it that night long after I am supposed to be asleep.

In June, Sherry wraps the pin in a small box, mailing it to me in a brown envelope with a graduation card. The pin is a pewter stick figure with a square head and outstretched arms. There's a silver dot in the center of the head that looks like an eye. The little man — I've always thought of it as male — is impish, whimsical, and quite possibly magical, although I have yet to find the right incantation.

The little man makes me laugh at a time when jewelry is laden with the weight of responsibility. "I think you're old enough to wear the cultured pearls," my grandmother says, as though there is still some doubt. The gold bracelet, the mustard-seed pendant, the turquoise ring are rites of passage. The little man is a wink. It is Sherry's giggle, her fast-moving, fast-thinking self, her bright voice telling me to wear bolder colors and go ahead and ask somebody to the Sadie Hawkins Day Dance.

Sherry?

The girl is gone. The letters are gone. I can't even remember now if she spelled her name with a *y* or an *i*. There is nothing but silence.

I hold the pin tightly, willing it to tell the story, but it is silent too. I was too scared to write to her parents when I found out and didn't know what to say. I have searched for her name on Google, knowing it isn't there. Sherry is a video loop in my mind, running like the Zapruder clip of John F. Kennedy in Dallas. Waving, smiling, then gone. Waving, smiling, then gone.

Other friends have been lost to time, but none like this, at least none that I know about. They rest gently in the nostalgia of "I wonder whatever happened to . . . ?" They may be contemplated over a glass of wine, filed under "Someday we'll have to get together."

Sherry and I were in school together for just eight months in the 1960s, and yet she is with me in my sixties. What would have happened if she hadn't moved away? Would we still be friends? Or was ours a comet friendship, destined to cool and vanish because we knew so little about each other and the world?

My mother used to say there are friends of the road, bonded through circumstances, and friends of the heart bonded forever. In 1963, I thought Sherry was both. Maybe I still do.

Life can feel like a train ride. It pulls into a station for a while, then zooms away with everything growing smaller behind it. The Buddhists say it is healthy to let go of the past and live in the moment. But the little man in my hand demands that I hang on tight to what I cannot grasp.

CHAPTER 15

Present Tense

Incoming!

The cell phone makes me jump. It has played the same syncopated synthesizer riff for years, and I should be used to it by now, not going into fight-or-flight mode, not feeling like ground zero for the big satellite in the sky, not wanting to hide from the great god of alleged modern convenience as it swoops into a clothing store dressing room, demanding interaction with the world, while I'm standing in my underwear.

I could ignore it, but don't. I never ignore it, except while driving, and sometimes not even then if the traffic is light. Who's calling? Why? Is there an emergency? Fingers fumble with stubborn pocketbook zippers as the tune keeps going and going like a synthesizer symphony. Why don't younger people have this problem? Why do their phones seem like extensions of their hands and their heads? Sometimes the receivers are invisible and a kid is talking to the air while carrying on a simultaneous conversation with the kid next to him, who is also talking to the air. And nobody feels strange.

Boom-chicka-chicka-chicka, Boom-chicka-chicka-chicka. Are people in adjacent dressing rooms thinking, "Who's the jerk with the bad music? Why didn't she pick *'Fur Elise'* or 'Yankee Doodle' like the rest of us?" There's some slim measure of pride in knowing I've never heard my *Boom-chicka* on anybody else's phone. Originality counts for something, even if it falls way short of cool.

Where IS the little son of a satellite? Not in the dedicated cell-phone pocket that purse manufacturers have designed for organized women to corral their technology. Not in the dedicated eyeglass pocket. Both empty. Phone and glasses in free fall. If I could find one, maybe I could see the other.

Reaching deep into the Kleenex lint, I feel pens, notepaper, and my address book. So last century, the address book, which not only has addresses and home phones written in it, but a few cell numbers. Everything in the book could go into the phone I can't find, and will someday when there is time to figure out how to get it in there and I'm ready for convergence.

The phone is buried in the makeup bag. I yank it out and flip it open on the last *chicka* to find, not a call, but a text message filling the screen. It's my first — a Happy Birthday note from the nieces. Very sweet. Make that *sa-weet* that two people under age 25 think I can handle this form of communication. Luckily they can't see me holding the phone as though it were a bomb.

Don't want to blow it. Don't want it to blow. Try to remember the fast-thumb cell-phone tutorial a teenage cousin gave the adults last Christmas. Should have taken notes. Push the green key? No. That makes everything disappear. Find the menu. Find the text function. Sounds like a really bad party, a text function.

I picture people in a banquet hall tapping out messages to each other over their rubber chickens.

Don't let the mind wander. Focus. Something about a code. Get me Dan Brown at home. Numbers stand for letters. A,B,C is 1,2,3. Unless it's not. I sit on the dressing-room bench, feel a draft, and talk to myself.

"How are we doing in here?" the clerk asks.

"Fine, just fine."

"Let me know if you need anything."

I need a 20-year-old, but there aren't any in the store because this is Coldwater Creek and the 20-year-olds are over at the Gap and American Eagle. I decide to call the nieces, cell to cell, and pull out the retro address book to look up their numbers. Not in there. Why? Don't know. Probably at home on a scrap of paper. Not sure where. So much for convergence.

I get dressed, drive home, sit at the big computer on the desk, and type an e-mail to the girls, thanking them for remembering. I do not mention that their text message went into the ether or that their aunt can't type on anything but a full-size, 10-finger keyboard that hasn't changed its layout much since it was invented in the 1800s. I do not mention that texting can kill people, and has, in highway and train accidents.

Warning of impending doom with gadgets is a sign of creeping geezerhood, possibly galloping geezerhood. It would be like channeling the grandparents who used to look at something as innocent as a hula hoop, raise a forefinger to heaven, and proclaim: "You could take an eye out with that thing."

I have never said that. Yet. But it could slip out. I worry about slippage in retirement, about sounding old, thinking old, getting old, and sitting on the bench of life, not quite sure what game is on the field, never mind the score. I worried about it the last few years at work, too, but was surrounded by smart newspaper people who were paid to know what was going on. They provided a sense of security, these techno wizards, these trendies who understood fashion, these intrepid souls who went to rock concerts without earplugs. I could walk up to any number of desks and grab a lifeline: "Psst. Know how to program this thing?" "Are bell bottoms back?" "Who's Beyoncé?"

Now there is a lot more alone time with Google. I stumble around an increasingly alien culture, often intimidated by progress, and wonder if every generation reaches that point where the past sounds like harmony and the present like static. *Zing, zing, zing* — the lights flash, the planet whirls, and the innovations fly at me like laser beams. I want to get it, but I cling to modernity by the fingernails.

"Do you bank online?" the smiling teller asks after passing a deposit receipt through his window. He's giving the day's product pitch. Other tellers are talking up online banking, too, informing customers that a trainer is available to sit down and show them how easy it is to go all electronic.

"Not yet," I tell him, folding the receipt into the wallet with the ATM withdrawal slips, feeling the reassurance of good old paper records that will be typed into the computer checkbook one by one on the weekend. It took several years for my husband to convince me that the computer is a much more efficient way to balance a checkbook than a handheld calculator. He is also pushing online banking, but not very hard.

"Why not yet?" the teller wants to know, politely insistent.

"Fear."

He laughs at the joke, not realizing it's also the truth. This man has never met an electronic device he didn't like. This man can text.

"We'll walk you through it right now," he says. "Then you'll go home, log on, and be all set."

I know better. I will go home, log on, get lost after clicking the wrong prompt, transposing numbers, forgetting codes, and sending the entire balance to the electric company. A call to the bank will inform me that the trainer is no longer available, and I'll be transferred to the 800 help line, where there are no human beings no matter how loudly I scream, "Operator!" or "Agent!" or bang the pound sign.

"Let me think about it."

ANOTHER CORNER OF THE modern world deferred. Not rejected — just awaiting further action and a day when I feel strong.

Perhaps on that same strong day when I send the money into cyberspace, I will boldly walk through an automated supermarket checkout line without making buzzers and lights go off because the machine can't read the product numbers on my stuff. I will embrace the talking scanner like an old pal, not caring how loud the robotic voice is when it announces every item in the basket and the price, not caring that it might as well be shouting, "SHE BOUGHT THE CHEETOS, LADIES AND GENTLEMEN. SHE HAS THE WILLPOWER OF A FLEA." I won't care that it's nobody's business who buys what discounted deodorant, who has athlete's foot — or worse — or that what people choose to eat, or not eat, should be a private matter between themselves and their blood-pressure machines. I will hold the Metamucil high for all to see and feel like a star on YouTube.

But for now, I want the line where the registers haven't learned to talk and the customers wait quietly to get processed by their own species, no matter how long it takes. For now, I avoid eye contact with the supermarket manager trying to entice people over to the robots that will put the cashiers out of work. "Come on, folks, give it a try," he says with a phony smile, looking like a sideshow barker as he waves a fistful of discount coupons available to any takers. "It's easy."

I figure he must know the guys at my bank.

There are few takers. It's a weekday afternoon, and the geezers are out. They like cashiers. They're doing exactly what I'm doing. Does the manager think I'm a geezer?

Maybe I should explain about the loud robotic voice, the general static in the marketplace, the slower learning curve, and the plan for eventual convergence. I'm not a Luddite. It's just that when somebody says "easy," the thing usually turns out to be hard.

"THIS IS FiOS. THIS IS BIG," the Verizon mailers announce, sending me to Google, where experts explain that the initials stand for the company's trademarked "Fiber Optic Service." John doesn't have to look anything up on Google. He is seven years younger and intuitive about technology. He can't wait to have the Verizon guy in the white truck come over and tie our telephone, television, and Internet service into one giant bundle that is supposed to work faster than Einstein's mind. He does not envision something going *fzzzzt* and blowing our connections to the outside world.

"It's a good deal," John says, even though neither of us can decipher the first bill. He has faith in the system. Comes the day I have faith in the system, it will be replaced by a faster, more confounding one that promises to make communications even "easier." But for now, at least, I know the current whatsis is earning us points with the nephew, who likes big, fast, electronic everything. He was the first in the family to get a plasma TV.

"That's next," John tells him on the upgraded phone, and I think, "Over my dead Zenith," which must have years of life left now that it's all FiOS-ed up. John wants more pixels, or something. He wants to see the nasal hairs of the football players. He fantasizes about a media room. I just want to see the ball on our modest old screen with its fat butt sitting unobtrusively on a shelf in a corner, preferably in a cabinet with doors.

Is this the broadcasting equivalent of not wanting to give up the handheld calculator? Is it the kind of recalcitrance that could drive a husband to a hottie with a loaded iPod, interactive home theatre, and surround sound?

"We can look," I say on the way to the big-box store.

Two minutes in, I want out. The place makes the automated supermarket line seem bucolic. Walls of televisions are coming at us, bright, loud, flashing, clashing. Limousine-length televisions. Room-high televisions. Televisions from outer space. Horror movies, volcanoes, baseball, football, golf, poker, talk shows, soaps, cops, docs, pets all playing at once, and I don't see any on/off switches. This is where Dante would go if he were writing today.

Our guide through the ninth circle is Claudia. She is one of the smartest clerks I have ever met in a big-box store or anywhere. She is MIT with piercings and spiked sling-backs. She walks fast on the waxed floor and never slips. I'm carefully padding behind her in tie shoes. She answers every question without hesitation. She has memorized the manuals. No, she has probably written the manuals. She talks faster than she walks, explaining plasma, LCD, HDMI, LED, Blu-ray, resolutions, contrast ratios, connectors, surge protectors, the V series, the S series, and the "refresh problem." She looks at me and says, "It'll be okay."

No it won't. I remember rabbit ears and I'm afraid of the phone. The scariest thing Claudia tells us is that our DVD player, purchased in 2004, is a relic and won't work with a new set.

"But we just got it," I whine. It's the newest entertainment innovation in our house, not counting whatever the guy in the white truck did to the wires. She shrugs a "that's technology for you" kind of shrug and says our stereo receiver is yesterday, too, and that the new ones are so much better and, yes, "easier" to hook up.

Our stereo receiver and CD player date back to 1995, when Claudia was in high school. She smiles the way I used to when parents and grandparents talked about the old Philco. Her smile tells me that CDs are on their way out, if they're not gone already, antiquated before I've mastered the little razor zipper gadget that takes off their cellophane packaging. CDs are over because playing round things on machines is like writing names in an address book. This is the age of uploading and downloading. So much simpler, really, than spinning — simpler if change doesn't make your head spin.

"Let's defer," I whisper to John. And we do because he's looking a little dazed himself as he mentally adds up price tags for "a system" after coming into the store thinking he'd replace a television. Buying one item is not possible in the age of convergence.

I want to stomp a tie shoe on the shiny floor and yell, "Make it stop! Everything was just fine the way it used to be," which is the second most fuddy-duddy pronouncement on the slippage chart, right after "You could take an eye out." I go quietly to the car and say nothing, but wish there were companies with the vision to continue manufacturing old innovations.

I wish television program directors didn't make shows move so fast, like video games, didn't jerk me around all those hospitals and *CSIs* (not to be confused with *NCIS*, which is the Navy, maybe). I subscribe to *TV Guide* and vow to plug in, or at least keep the names straight, following the idols, the dancers, and the island dwellers voted up, out, or off.

I don't. I identify most with *Life on Mars*, and ABC cancelled that one. Usually I just turn on the classical music channel, which is the best thing about FiOS TV. Pictures of composers and performers, and sometimes a brief history about a piece, appear on the screen as the music plays. It's radio with pictures and provides perfect non-commercial background music for reading. Now, *that's* innovation.

Am I fighting the modern world? Refusing to learn? Is this the first stage of rigor mortis, or is it a quiet stand for common sense? It seems to be evaporating, common sense, but the techno-wizard marketers don't notice. They're too busy inventing the next generation of something purchased a half-dozen models ago that I haven't finished reading the instruction booklets for yet. They're too busy solving problems I didn't know existed.

"The CVI coffeemaker eliminates concerns about the cleanliness of traditional guestroom coffeepots, brew baskets, and coffee mugs," says the sign in an Ithaca hotel room. "It's the most sanitary way we know to provide you with a great cup of coffee in the comfort of your room."

The sign raises more concerns than it eliminates, because John and I have never worried about the cleanliness of traditional guestroom coffeepots, brew baskets, and coffee mugs. Now we're thinking that God-knows-what may have gone down the gullet to God-knows-where over the past couple of decades, and a vacation could kill us. Another raised concern is that this hotel monument to cleanliness, with its individually wrapped paper cups and state-of-the-art drip mechanism, is plugged into the room's only available outlet, which happens to be on the bathroom counter next to the toilet.

We defer and look for a Starbucks, which is, of course, "wired." The people wearing ear pieces, working their phones and BlackBerrys, and tapping on laptops while lapping froth all seem to know what they're doing and are not bothered by convergence. They are not bothered by the illogic of a drink menu that has innovated "small," "medium," and "large" into "tall," "grande," and "venti" — with the smallest being 12 ounces. Someone who wants a standard eight-ounce cuppa joe is supposed to ask for a "short," according to an Internet site, quicksilverweb.net, dedicated to all things Starbucks. But how would customers know that if it's usually not on the menu board? And how did coffee get to be so complicated that it has to be explained on a computer?

Anyone irritated by such things is probably a cranky coot who should stay home and drink instant decaf. I plop into a big, soft chair, chomp on a biscotti, and try not to be irritated, try not to think. But I spot a water bottle, and backward slips the mind.

Water has been innovated so far beyond the dripping kitchen tap that it might as well be orbiting Pluto, which is where the H_2O ad copywriters probably live. How else to explain a supermarket label announcing that the product is "infused with raspberry essence," or "naturale aqua minerale from Tuscany," or "born beneath the Catskill Mountains in velvety smooth spring water with exceptional virginity"?

I wonder if there is such a thing as "average" virginity. How about an H_2O that's been around and works the street in fishnet stockings? Would they call it just plain "ho"?

INCOMING!

This time it's the land phone going off in the house, so I know where to find it. But the answering machine is quicker, and I'm glad, because the call is a recorded message pitching an automobile warranty. It's the third robocall of the day. The others came from a credit-card company and a candidate for state rep, but they had the decency to disconnect when I slammed down the receiver. This one keeps talking.

I bang the receiver a couple of times and still can't get rid of the voice. I try hitting the "erase" button on the machine, but the mechanical voice continues to blast out of the speaker, oblivious to the redundancy of a recording being recorded after another recording tells it to leave a message. I hit "skip" "volume," and "stop." Nothing. I move on to the mystery buttons I never touch — "memo," "review," "in use charge/hold," and "locator/ intercom." Still nothing. I pick up the machine and pound it against the desk. It's him or me.

Silence. But only because the recorded voice has finished repeating the 800-number three times. Don't these people know I'm not listening? Hasn't someone in marketing school ever mentioned that they shouldn't alienate the buying public?

I close my eyes and remember the old black, rotary-dial phone in the living room, next to my mother's chair. It did absolutely nothing but ring, and it couldn't travel. I remember stores and elevators without Musak, waiting rooms without televisions, and highways and shopping centers without video billboards. I remember walking past magazine racks and seeing Mary Tyler Moore and Peter Falk on the covers instead of what seems like an assembly line of stars churned out new every week and arriving without their clothes.

That's strike three on the slippage chart, unless I'm up to four. Thinking people look naked, and being shocked by 12-year-olds in push-up bras, is my mother saying I looked like a tramp in a straight skirt and a reversed cardigan sweater worn buttoned up the back. We used to call them "tight skirts" and saw them on *American Bandstand*.

But is it really the same? Why does it seem so different now?

I'm not LinkedIn, I don't Twitter or get Tweets, and I got on Facebook by mistake while trying to send an e-mail to somebody who was in there on purpose. Now I get e-mails from strangers who want to be my friends. Trying to take my name off the site, I found another Susan Trausch pictured with two children. She's not me. Unless she is.

Were people happier when things moved more slowly or were they deprived? If I could push a button and go back to the past, would I? Probably not. But there are days, maybe a little part of every day, when I'd sure like to drop in for a long visit.

CHAPTER 16

2008: KA-BOOM!

What was THAT?

The stock market.

Holy shit!

Relax.

How?

Don't think about your IRA.

Aren't you thinking about it?

No.

Why not? You're the left brain. You're supposed to do numbers.

I do logic.

The entire global economy is teetering on the rim of the fiscal toilet seat, and you're okay with this, logically?

I'm staying balanced, focused, riding out the crisis.

The crisis. Exactly. We're having a crisis here. Just like 1929.

Not like 1929.

Like what then? 1970? 2001?

Like 2008.

Meaning nobody's ever seen one like this before, and you can't explain it either.

The market went down.

Thank you.

And it will go back up.

When?

Nobody knows.

And in the meantime?

You hang in there. You don't panic.

I don't go to Starbucks and get a job as a barista?

Do you want to go to Starbucks and get a job as a barista?

No.

Do you want to go back into the newspaper business?

What newspaper business?

Then suck it up and stop whining.

I'm scared.

Again.

I've got a right to be scared. Lehman Brothers, Merrill Lynch, AIG, Citibank, the auto industry, Washington, the world. They're all scared, all groping. Groping!

Your parents and grandparents groped through the Great Depression.

Why do you think I'm scared?

They made it, didn't they?

And talked about it endlessly at family dinners. Forks waving, mouths full: "You kids don't know how bad the bad times were!"

They were right. You don't know.

But I feel like I know. Their 1930s loomed over my 1950s like a buzzard at a banquet. And their decade is still here.

They were teaching you to appreciate what you have.

And never to forget that it can all go "*poof!*" no matter how good things seem.

It hasn't all gone "poof!"

2008 — The Year of the Buzzard. Payback time for not keeping a year's supply of canned goods in the pantry, for not buying the cheap toilet paper, for having the gall to retire early.

Stop looking backwards. You'll strain your neck.

It's the future I'm worried about.

Nobody can be sure of the future. We went through all that in Chapter 12.

That's supposed to cheer me up?

You want guarantees. There aren't any.

I feel like I missed a signal somewhere.

So does Wall Street.

I used to be a business reporter, but the words swirl around and I can't grasp the core. Secondary mortgage market, collateralized debt obligations, housing bubble, hedge funds, credit crunch, TARP.

You don't have to explain it. Just get through it.

But what am I'm supposed to DO? Buy? Sell? Punt? Acquire a marketable skill?

Wait until things settle.

I'm no good at waiting.

Keep your head down and write.

Is that still a marketable skill?

What happened to being philosophical about money?

That was back when there was more of it, back before Alan Greenspan's face was on the front page of the *New York Times* looking like he wished he'd put everything in the mattress.

Forget Alan Greenspan. Think Warren Buffett.

Does he have an IRA?

He has confidence, vision, brio.

And a couple billion in the bank.

This is not about billions in the bank.

How would you know? You don't even shop.

This is about staying calm.

That's what Herbert Hoover said.

This is about thinking 10 years out and not following the daily Dow Jones averages as though they were a local sports team.

Go mutual funds! Go bonds! DEE-fense! DEE-fense! DEE-fense!

You're not listening.

The headlines read like *Tales from the Crypt.*

Stop reading the headlines.

Can't help it. I pick up the papers and there they are: "YOUR MONEY RUN AMOK!" "SHOCK WAVES!" and "WHO WILL BE NEXT?"

Focus on some good news.

Like what?

You're paying your mortgage.

In a world gone bonkers.

It'll pass.

Like gas?

Like everything passes. And comes around again.

The illogic doesn't get to you?

No.

Not even when the stock market tanks yet again two months after the big ka-boom just because the National Bureau of Economic Research announces the country is "officially" in a recession? I mean, Duh! The market didn't know this?

The market overreacts. Just like some people.

So, why didn't the National Bureau of Economic Research give us the news while singing "Happy Days Are Here Again"?

Government statisticians are not known for their zany streak.

Speaking of zany, where does Gucci get off running ads for $895 green snakeskin Christmas sneakers with black and red trim? Isn't that a little insensitive?

Gucci will always be Gucci, and there will always be a buyer.

And what about MasterCard sending a letter about lowering my credit ceiling a couple thousand bucks because I'm not spending enough?

Consider it a compliment.

It felt like an insult.

Your relatives with the year's supply of canned goods and cheap toilet paper are smiling.

I'm not.

Take a deep breath.

I'd rather hyperventilate.

Whatever.

I thought I was doing everything right. The 401k, the savings account, the employee stock options, the steady job, the modest house, playing by the rules, and then—

Ka-boom!

Yeah.

You'll regroup.

You're sure about that?

You're alive, you're healthy, you've got a brain, and the world is in this together.

Except for Gucci.

Shut up and type.

CHAPTER 17

The Open Window

Fresh air is the answer. It doesn't matter what the question is. I pull the cord of the venetian blind, raise the sash, and breathe. It clears the brain, calms the crazies, and focuses the eye on the tree-lined horizon, away from gadgets, digits, clutter, confusion, fear. It is an exquisite retirement moment that could never have happened at the office because my cubicles rarely had a window. And if they did have one, it was sealed shut.

Most windows are sealed shut in the business world. This is supposed to maintain a "climate-controlled environment," which sounds like a good idea until people try to work in it and fidget their productivity away obsessed with the need for air — warmer air, colder air, more humid air, real air. A thermostat is a rarity, and if there is one on the wall, it is usually locked up as tightly as the windows. Climate-controlled environments are controlled by someone else, and the people obsessed with the need for air spend much of the day trying to find out who that person is.

On a cumulative average, I probably wasted one or two years of a journalism career searching for central control and griping to plant managers, maintenance supervisors, and their assistants about the air blowing like a blast furnace or an arctic wind, or not blowing at all, from the ceiling and window vents that were supposed to provide comfort in times of employment. The best I got was, "We'll send somebody up."

The somebody who came up was never the Air Czar, but rather a harried, short-sleeved, hourly-wage maintenance guy, understandably weary from listening to people complain about a system that someone else controlled and that he couldn't fix because it was designed for buildingwide efficiency rather than the comfort of a single room.

"If we turn the heat down in this department, advertising is going to freeze," he'd say, holding a hand over the vent on a mild winter day and noting that the temperature was "a little warm," but still "in the normal range" according to readings taken with a thermometer carried in his shirt pocket. The reading would be "normal" on a chilly summer day, too, when the room was pronounced "a little cool," even if people were wearing turtlenecks.

Seasons in the office seem to follow an Australian calendar and reinforce the message in the withering potted plants, the odd-tasting water from the drinking fountain, the artificial light that is too harsh or too dim, and the eerie deadening of most outdoor sound, save the occasional buzzing of a disoriented fly, sucked in through a vent and slamming itself against the walls, desperate to find its way out again. The message could be inscribed in stone over the front door: *Life inside these walls bears no relation to the natural world.*

That's why I love opening windows now simply because I can. That's why I'm a weather nut, sniffing the air, eager for whatever is coming next. I go outside and sniff more deeply, watching a groundhog in the back field emerge from his hole and do the same. Are we catching the scent of rain or the more acrid whiff of snow? I look up at the fast-moving clouds, feel the wind shifting, and wait — curious, alert, connected. The woodchuck and I know that seasons begin in subtleties. We feel it from the grass blades up. Long before the brilliant colors of autumn, there is a dryness in the plants and a hint of decay rising from the garden soil. Long before daffodils, there is the smell of thawing earth and the beginnings of barely perceptible buds on the trees.

No more gatekeepers between me and the climate. No more relegating the outdoors to prescribed blocks of time — the vacation, the weekend, the rare lunch-hour walk. Nature is not what I pass through in a hurry to get to someplace more important. It isn't the problem that fouls the commute, making me late or absent, because the driveway snow is too deep to shovel and the plow is on its way but slowed by a storm.

"I got in," the boss would snap into the phone, flattening the drifts.

Nothing ruins a good snow day now. I'm out taking pictures of it, the higher the better. Shoveling is a meditation — scoop, lift with the knees, toss. The shovel is small and light. The snow is often fluffy and light, and if it's heavy, there are more scoops, or I can wait until it melts.

One, two, three. One, two, three. It's a winter waltz. Up the walk to the front steps. Up the steps to the door. Back down to square off the ragged edges. One, two, three. One, two, three.

I walk into the backyard to measure the drifts against knee-high boots. Ankle, shin, over the top to the thigh. It's important to know what fell where, to take a photo of the icicles hanging from the house, the white caps mounded on the bird feeders, the herb garden buried except for a defiant sprig of thyme, and the sun making a golden path into the neighbor's yard.

The deep-snow winters are the best, reminding me of childhood winters when I wouldn't come inside until my feet turned numb. Boots are a lot better today, but the snow is as fascinating as it always was, silently transforming the landscape with soft flakes, or roaring it white in a howler.

What's the weather going to do? Where's the snow line, the rain line? How much of each will we get? When? I can find out, more or less, because of the weather patterns, satellite tracking, and maps. The presumed unpredictability of climate is a well-marked trail compared to the crooked little heart of the stock market.

I check Weather Underground on the Internet a couple times a day, I study the week's forecast, the local radar, the regional and national radar, and I click on "animate" for all three to make the rain and snow fronts move across the U.S. map. Oh, the feeling of power in making the fronts move!

If a storm is coming, I listen to the weather people on the radio every 10 minutes to find out if it's inside Route 495 yet. I go to the National Weather Service Web site and mess with their maps. I follow the snow, the rain, the ice, the hurricanes making landfall or blowing out to sea, the Bermuda highs, the tropical depressions, the Canadian air masses, the Atlantic, the Pacific, Indonesia, El Niño, La Niña, and sunspots.

Some people might be thinking "She's got way too much time on her hands and needs a life." But nature is a life too often ignored. These people should look outside, walk outside, and sit in a park in the middle of the afternoon and just listen. The sound of birds, squirrels, frogs, leaves, and streams can lower the blood pressure and lift the spirit. Invisible feet scurrying through the brush tell the story of cycles that have been followed for thousands of years and will be followed for thousands more. Taking time to absorb that in a fast-lane culture with a cracked economy is not sitting around doing nothing. It's not about resting in a rocking chair and simply enjoying the view. Breaking the hermetic seal between man's business and nature's is to know that the barrier was an illusion and that we are all part of a much larger space.

I look out and see deer in the yard. They seem to materialize the way the Starship *Enterprise* crew did on the old *Star Trek* show. One second, the lawn is empty. Look up again, and there are four deer, or six, or 10. They arrive without a sound to nibble the grass, the apples, the bushes. Not even their nibbling makes a noise. A buck watches the house while the others eat. I know he's staring at me, or at least smelling the human at the window. He would not tolerate the human coming any closer. I've tried to be as quiet as the deer while stepping out on the back porch, but in an instant they are gone, vanishing into the woods as quietly as they came.

They can appear at any time of day, so I look up from the computer often, hoping to catch their entrance. Driving into the garage at night, I shine the high beam on the yard for a deer check and quickly snap off the lights if they are there so they won't be spooked.

Too many deer in the woods, the wildlife experts say, and culling the herds is supposed to be a good thing. "Culling" is a euphemism for "killing." The experts are right, and in *The Yearling*, Marjorie Kinnan Rawlings wrote the story long ago, but I could never kill one of these graceful, magical animals. I've come to know them, or think I do — the doe with the twin fawns, the buck and his family, the lone buck, the teenagers chasing each other, the reunion picnic that brings the herd. Maybe they're not the same deer every time. Who can tell for sure? I do know that those moments when the buck and I stare at each other seem electric. I don't move, don't want to break the spell.

I watch skunks, too, even though they are not so magical or silent. They are still riveting as they ripple across the grass to munch bugs and sunflower seeds under the bird feeders. I hear them digging and snuffling up beetles. They are loners, usually arriving one at a time at night. I turn on the yard light to see if it's a black skunk with the white stripe or a white one with a black stripe. We call them all "Pepé Le Pew." They don't care what we call them, or fret about the light. They don't look up to stare warily at humans. They just keep eating. They know they've got the bomb.

I look out the window one summer afternoon and see a bald cardinal amid the beauty flying around the feeders. I get the binoculars and look again. He's still there, a freak with a cardinal body and beak, the dramatic scarlet color, but not one feather on his head, which is a dead gray and missing the trademark crest. Is he diseased, healing from an attack? Will he freeze in the winter? Should I try to take him to the New England Wildlife Center?

The Web site of the Cornell Lab of Ornithology tells me other people have reported bald birds and attributes the condition to an "abnormal molt" or maybe mites. Nobody knows the exact cause, but the feathers will grow back. Does the bird know this? Is he impatient to be gorgeous once again? Does he seek out his reflection in every shiny surface, looking for the first signs of growth? Does he seem less of a bird to the others? No, neither he nor the rest of the flock appear to be aware that he's *different*. So, why should I?

A phoebe builds a nest on the ceiling light in the storage area under the porch. I watch her through the laundry-room window as she brings food to three growing young ones. First they are just cheeps barely audible from the nest. Over the weeks, the tips of beaks emerge, then gaping mouths, then squirming whole birds vying to get the mouthful of bugs from their mother. She flies in and out of the storage area most of the day, perching on the edge of the crowded nest to feed the brood.

John and I feel like grandparents, call them "Phoebe and the Phoebettes," and hope to be there at the laundry-room window for the first flight. I worry that one of the birds will get shoved out in all the jostling for food. I want to put pillows on the cement floor. John tells me to get a grip. "They're birds," he says. "They know what to do."

And they do, taking off one morning just before I get to the window. I hear the squawking and flapping. Mama is calling her sharp, quick little "pheebee" from a growing distance, and the nest is empty.

I try to spot them in the yard, but can't, and yell good-bye anyway, giving them a double thumbs-up. It's a fine launch, I think, until I turn back to the house and see the tiny body of a lifeless bird on the mat outside the laundry-room door. How had I missed it? And had I killed it, hitting it with the door in the rush to get outside? I don't remember the dismal thud of feathers hitting glass, but I wasn't paying attention.

I stare down at the dead bird lying on its back and cry harder than I have in years. All those weeks, all the care, all that watching.

John comes out and bends down to look. He picks it up gently with a garden trowel and studies the feathers. "It's not one of the phoebes," he says with a hand on my shoulder. "It's a sparrow."

I feel relief for a microsecond. It's not one of "our" birds. The phoebettes are all flying and safe. It's okay. But no, the tears keep coming. It's not okay. A young lost bird is still a bird lost, and maybe on its first flight too. Cry for one, cry for them all.

ON A BROILING, still July afternoon when the porch thermometer reads 100, I see a white bird standing on the sidewalk across the road. Is it a seagull? No, too small. A snowy owl? No, wrong season.

I go out the front door slowly to get closer. The bird walks toward me, crosses the road and comes up the driveway. It is a beautiful dove and shows no fear. I'm the one afraid that it's somebody's pet, hurt, and unable to fly. But as if to answer that thought, it raises its wings and glides up to the peak of the roof, where it sits and preens. I worry that it's hungry and shake a handful of sunflower seeds. I run over to the hose and fill up the birdbath to let it know it can drink and cool off. It is not interested. It is just fine. It flies up toward the sun, heads out over the field, and is gone.

Flocks of gray mourning doves come into the yard every day, but there had never been a white dove, and there hasn't been one since. Was it real or was I hallucinating in the heat? How could a bird be that calm? I wonder if it was the spirit of peace, making its rounds, offering sustenance to man. I look up into the sky and say, "Thank you."

↦ CHAPTER 18 ↤

That New Old Gang of Mine

"WE'LL KEEP IN TOUCH," people say after cleaning out their desks, after hugs and good-byes. "We'll do lunch."

Some do, but most don't. Scattering seems to be the natural way of large groups breaking up — students who've gone through high school and graduated, assembly-line workers who have stood side by side and retired, or journalists who have put out a newspaper for decades and left on the economic tide.

Where did they go, these colleagues who left the paper around the same time I did, whose faces had once been as familiar as relatives? What were they doing? It was 2009, going on four years out and I needed a reunion. Not a room full of people — I was no good at retiree dinners. I wanted to talk, one-on-one, wanted to stop the movie, study a freeze-frame, ask for a synopsis, get a review. Were they still euphoric? Having crazy days, fulfilling days? Were they soaring, stumbling, finding their way? Groping?

At the newspaper, we had known each other by our titles, our roles, our carefully crafted words. We'd known each other by our slammed doors and voices barking into phones, by our work talk, work jokes, office politics, gossip, achievements, and daily products. But what do we become when all that stops? Hello? I'll show you my retirement if you show me yours.

"SPENT ALL MY RETIREMENT MONEY, got divorced, learned to enjoy cleaning up bodily fluids," the 59-year-old man writes in answer to my e-mail.

He is studying to be a nurse. At the *Globe*, he'd been a production editor for several sections — the last pair of eyes on the pages before they went to press. But he's as good at science and math as he is at editing, and he wants a career that makes him feel more "useful."

We meet in the Borders Café in Braintree. A thick medical book is open in front of him on the table. He is preparing for an exam that will cover endocrinology, hypertension, and mental health.

"I'm going into the future flat, busted broke," he says, his soft voice matter-of-fact. His 401k and severance package have gone into a divorce settlement and into paying off credit-card debt that ballooned during his marriage. He has moved from a home in the suburbs to a rented room in Boston, where he gets by on what's left of his savings, a student loan, and unemployment checks.

"I don't regret a thing," he says, smiling. He is looking forward to receiving his associate's degree in nursing at the end of the year and taking the board exam. He wants to work in acute care in the United States before joining Doctors Without Borders in Haiti, West Africa, or Cameroon. He is studying French to prepare for going overseas.

Being an older white guy makes him a rarity at Roxbury

Community College, where fellow students are younger, black, and come from places like Zambia, Nigeria, Jamaica, Haiti, and the Democratic Republic of Congo. He helps them with American idioms and grammar. They teach him about the world.

"I go to school with people who have had malaria," he says, "people who used to herd goats back home. I've learned that the life expectancy in Zambia is only 38."

He knows what he wants to do and that he can get by on very little to reach his goal. "I can always get a job typing," he says. "I can pump gas. I can survive. I'm joyful and happy, and that's a surprise. I'm content."

"I've stopped drinking," she says. "I'm in AA."

For 36 years, she had been an administrative manager extraordinaire. Office moves, paint jobs, remodeling, payrolls, international itineraries, currency-exchange totals on expense accounts, newspaper logistics at a national political convention, executive egos — anything requiring the organizational skills of a stage manager at a circus, she was there: warm, funny, efficient, and beautiful, getting it done.

After retiring, she took on the hardest job of her life — managing herself. The circus had left town. The pulse of a frantic day no longer dictated her schedule, no longer made it okay to open the bottle of wine "to relax."

"I was drinking more and more," she says over lunch, recalling how she started sneaking wine, hiding it from her husband, and feeling out of control. "I'd be into a second bottle some nights. I was drinking every day."

On Easter Sunday, 2008, at age 58, she quit. "I was making dinner and drinking," she remembers. "I don't know how many glasses I had. The family was there. And all of a sudden it was so clear to me what I was doing. It was like *bong!* I looked ahead and could see where my life was going. I knew I had to stop. I was sick of this. I went into the bedroom and cried. I called the family in one by one and told them I had a drinking problem and that I was going to get help. My father said, 'You'll do it. I know you will.'"

Four days after our lunch, she would attend an AA ceremony to get the pin honoring her first year of staying sober. Her family would be there. Her father, who had died the previous year, would be there too, very much in her heart.

She says she would not have been able to stop drinking if she hadn't retired, which allowed her to move to a town beyond commuting distance, a town where nobody knew her. She doesn't miss an AA meeting, and her biggest fear is slipping. "I've heard people tell their stories. They stay sober for 20 years. Then they stop going to meetings and think they can have a drink."

She is thinking about going back to school, finding a part-time job, volunteering, "doing more." She describes tennis, golf, and the gym as "fillers" in a retiree's life, not substance.

"I want to go to bed at night and know I've accomplished something and want it to be more than a round of golf," she says, adding that she is optimistic about finding that something as long as alcohol isn't clouding her mind. "If I have that under control, the rest of my life is working."

THE LEARNING CURVE WENT STRAIGHT UP for the 62-year-old man who took a management job in communications after 32 years at the paper. The first thing he learned was that journalism is not communications — just one narrow piece of it. Journalism is a laser, powered by a deadline, focused on the clarity of the printed word. Communications is diffused light, often filtered through committees, and months can pass before anything is put on paper.

"I realized how task-oriented journalism is compared to strategic thinking," he says. "I missed knowing exactly what to do. At the newspaper, I knew who to call, what to write, what was expected. I wrote it or edited it and got it in the paper. There is a lot more nuance here. I have to be careful. We coordinate a media plan. We collaborate. We reach a consensus. We reach many *consensi*."

He laughs, adding, "Sometimes collaboration stinks."

He has had to become more tech savvy in his job of disseminating information to the news media, public policy makers, and think-tank members. The office atmosphere is more formal, and he commutes in the mainstream rush hour, what he calls, "the maw of the lemmings," to get to his desk by 8:30 A.M. — a time when many journalists are just getting out of the shower.

"I do feel challenged," he says. "I'm glad I forced myself to do something different, to get off my journalistic butt and try something new."

His newspaper career was lived mostly for the love of it in the best of times for that medium. What he does now as he saves for retirement and a son's college tuition is more like putting his shoulder to the wheel. But, then, work isn't supposed to be easy, is it? He quotes the put-down a *Globe* editor used to snap at reporters who complained about tough assignments: "That's why they call it work."

"IT'S LOW PAY, LOW STATUS, and lots of fun," says the man working as a part-time food-products demonstrator for a super-market chain.

He had been the production editor on the Sunday magazine for 27 years and worked with the intensity of an air traffic con-troller. He was the man who bolted for the train at the end of the day with equal intensity. Head down, gray ponytail bounc-ing against his slightly bent back, briefcase bulging with work, he stopped for no one. It took him two years and psychological counseling before he could build up the courage to quit his pres-sured job. He was "scared shitless" to let go of the identity.

At age 65, nearly four years after ditching the briefcase and the persona that had no time for small talk, he is being paid to chat up grocery-store shoppers three days a week. He is the skillet guy, the cookie and goodie guy, tempting passersby with cheese crackers, frozen breakfast munchies, confections made with evaporated milk, and other stuff they hadn't thought of buying until he says, "Hi. Want to give it a try?"

"It's a little like speed dating," he says with his deadpan deliv-ery. "You try to get people interested, get them to buy the prod-uct."

He wears a name tag and an apron and stands behind a table. He got the job on a whim after watching a demonstrator and asking about the work. "I like to talk to strangers," he says.

Sharing coffee with him and his wife on his day off, I urge him to do a piece about the grocery-store gig and to get back to writing the terrific essays the paper used to run whenever he had time to write them. But he shakes his head. He is living in the present, and the present will get polluted if he takes notes. No more pressure.

His wife feels the same about her photography and has resisted turning her art into a production schedule by having pictures published on calendars and cards. "At our age, there's a choice," she says. "There's having to produce something versus getting up in the morning and being happy."

She has been an entrepreneur with many jobs — setting up a town bookmobile, working as a physical therapist, running a shop. Now retired, she volunteers at a school library, runs a teen photo club, writes poetry, and researches genealogy. Together she and her husband have volunteered as apprentice lighthouse keepers, and he has assisted tourists in the area visitors' center. He is also an ardent fisherman, skier, and kayaker, but too much leisure makes him "itchy." Although his wife is content to follow her bliss, he wants to be paid for a job, no matter how small. It's not about the money — not even in a bad economy — for they have always lived frugally. He wants the validation of having expertise and the acknowledgment that he has done a day's work.

"You have a different incentive when you're being paid," he says. "And working makes time off more valuable. Having this funky grocery-store job lets me enjoy a day like yesterday. I read a book, read the entire *New Yorker*, and wrote e-mails. The job gives me structure. There's no bad work."

"I HAD TO FIND SOMETHING TO DO or I would have wound up in McLean's," says the woman referring to McLean Hospital, a psychiatric facility. She thought she was more than ready for free time after 24 years as a reporter and editor. She had a long list of home projects, lots of friends, loved sports, and was sure she didn't want to turn 60 in the office. But the house was way too quiet.

"I remember coming down the stairs one day, sitting on the bottom step, and bursting into tears. I needed colleagues. I needed someplace to go. I felt there should be a point to my existence, some bigger point than just amusing myself."

She took a job as a government press secretary, working for what reporters consider *the other side*, the place to mine for investigative pieces on waste, fraud, and abuse. But her real-world civics lesson is showing her just the opposite. The public servant mindset is: work, work, work.

Our meeting is the first time she has been out of the building for lunch since taking the job. She is the only former colleague I talk with who keeps lunch under an hour (most went two or three), and the only one who doesn't have time for coffee. And we meet on what she calls her "relaxed day."

Is this job maybe too much of a good thing? She is thinking about going part-time instead of being on call 24/7. She is figuring out what she needs and doesn't need in her post-*Globe* life, finding her equilibrium somewhere between isolation and overload. Leaving the newspaper allowed her time to experience both. "I know myself much better now," she says, waving good-bye and hurrying back to work.

A FORMER NEWSROOM SECRETARY is still searching. "What's hard is not knowing where I fit anymore," she says. "I don't feel fulfilled. I get a pension check but don't feel like I've earned it."

She has done volunteer work at a homeless shelter but found it frustrating because "there were so many volunteers that I didn't feel useful." She has sold tickets at a movie theatre, applied to work for the U.S. Census Bureau, and is pursuing leads on being an events coordinator. "There's not enough going on to fill the day intellectually," she says.

The economy has slashed her savings, and like many people, she no longer opens her investment statements. She is also thinking about relocating, possibly to Florida, where the cost of living is lower.

Meanwhile, she does some traveling, reads, visits friends locally, and combats what she calls her "lack of discipline and focus" by getting up and out in the morning, dressed nicely and wearing makeup.

"You can't let yourself go," she says. "And you don't want to sit yourself in front of the box watching shows and wasting the day. Not working is lovely, but retirement is work. You have to put energy into it."

THE FORMER THEATRE CRITIC at the paper worries that he's running out of energy and says what has surprised him most about retirement is "the disappearance of adrenaline." He's had no trouble finding freelance work, which he does for the *Globe*, other publications, and radio. But he's not getting at bigger projects.

"I set the bar high for retirement," he says. "I planned to write books. I thought developing a writing schedule would be a breeze. I'd set aside two hours a day and do it. But I haven't. The dog gets walked four times a day. I ask myself, 'Do I need to go shopping?' And I say, 'Yeah, I guess I do need to go shopping.' I don't have a deadline, and the *Globe* made me an absolute deadline junkie."

He's found that it's not so easy now getting people to return his calls. Theatre people get back to him, but the book-publishing people, the places where he'd like to explore reinvention or expansion beyond what he has done, are not quick to respond.

"There's an ego adjustment for sure," he says.

NOT SO FOR THE NEWSROOM EXECUTIVE who shed her old management skin like a heavy coat on a hot day.

"I assumed it would matter that I wasn't in charge of something," she says, "It had been such a way of life."

But at 61, after being an editor for 32 years, she is working four volunteer jobs and learning Spanish. And when the Spanish teacher went around the room in the first class asking the great American question ("What do you do?"), she did not say what she used to be. She said, "I'm a volunteer," and the answer felt good.

The woman is one of eight workers in the kitchen of a homeless women's shelter. "I have the pancake franchise," she says. "I like knowing that there is something I can do for people and that I can do it right now. I can make pancakes and take them into the dining room on a cart."

She is also volunteering as a patient ombudsman at a nursing home, packing bags of groceries for an elder-service food program, and tutoring high-school students who are headed for college. I ask whether she would have felt the same sense of doing for people in her old life if she had assigned a reporter to write about these volunteer programs and she had put the story on the front page.

She shakes her head. "The difference is like being a doctor who works for years in a Mass. General lab in pediatric oncology research and then goes out and works one-on-one with kids who have cancer."

She started looking into volunteer possibilities before leaving the *Globe* with an executive severance package. She sees retirement as "a time to pay back." "The challenge," she says, "was to take that pile of money and use it to put together a bunch of things that were altruistic."

She describes her newspaper job as a bit like being a hockey goalie: "I'd strap on my skates and let the day come at me. It was almost automatic." In retirement, the day unfolds. "It's this wide-open vista," she says. "The day is about discovering whatever is out there."

THE FORMER MUSIC CRITIC has discovered music.

"I've learned a whole side of the business I didn't know," he says of his board membership overseeing an orchestral and choral performance group — a position that would have been considered a conflict of interest if he held it as a reviewer. He has learned about fund-raising, about how expensive a concert is to produce, about how hard an organization works, and why a performance can't always be as stellar as a critic might demand.

"I see a much bigger picture now," he says. "Performers, sponsors, and critics are all part of a giant interactive ecology."

He worked at the *Globe* for 33 years and hasn't written a review since leaving it. "I didn't want that to be my only relationship to music and to people who make music," he explains. He gives talks before concerts, writes magazine pieces and program notes, teaches, and provides content for podcasts on the Boston Symphony Orchestra's Web site.

"The wall is gone," he says of his relationship with music people who no longer view him as Mr. *Globe* Reviewer. "People are more frank, more open."

He has a fuller personal life, too. "I used to meet my friends at intermission," he says, giving me a tour of his remodeled home in Dorchester where he and his partner like to cook, entertain, or just watch movies.

"Last Saturday night, I decided to stay in," he says, recalling the years when that would have been impossible. "It was so good to know I didn't have to go anywhere. I can't imagine a happier post-*Globe* life."

Neither can the former arts pages editor who is studying art. He is taking classes, going to open studios, and learning to draw. He is finding the joy that comes with space, time, and quiet, seeking what he calls "a sense of completion."

At the *Globe*, he had been an intense, demanding boss, known for blowing up if a piece or a page wasn't right. Now all that is a long time ago.

"I'm way more relaxed," he says over a plate of oysters at Legal Sea Foods in Cambridge on an icy night in early March. "I live in the present. It is so solid. I didn't experience that as fully when I was working. I was more focused on stuff."

At 64, he is focused on the journey to the heart of things, to the soul, the great "ah-ha!" "It's about finding out what it is you were somehow meant to be," he says, noting that in his first art class, he knew he had found it. Journalism had been a fine, fascinating livelihood. But art is passion, growth, possibility, and challenge. He wants to go as far as a developing talent might take him.

Travel has become a passion, too, taking him to see great art and the planet. Travel had not happened before because of his flying phobia. His wife and son would go on vacations without him. He was determined to change that when he left the *Globe* and enrolled in a "fearless flying" course. It dissolved his anxiety through relaxation techniques and the redirection of negative thoughts. His new life itinerary has included London, Tuscany, Denmark, and Hungary.

"I get up in the morning and feel the promise of the day," he says. "I feel a stronger connection to myself, to others, and to the world. I feel more aligned."

THE FORMER ROCK-MUSIC CRITIC is getting eight hours of sleep a night, going to the gym, and concentrating on being a single parent to his 20-year-old son, who has autism. The young man is showing promise as an artist and has sold a painting.

"I'm putting a lot of energy into my kid," he says. "I'm planning to have a show for his work. I want to launch his career."

There wasn't time for that when he was covering as many as 250 shows a year and working late nights that turned into mornings. He had created the rock beat at the *Globe* and was toasted at three lavish Boston retirement parties when he left the paper — U2's Bono came to one of them.

He retired because he felt he was "presiding at two wakes" — the newspaper industry and the music business as he had known it before digital sound and hip-hop ruled, before the likes of Tom Petty, Mick Jagger, and Steven Tyler became the grand old men of rock, doing tours to sing their greatest hits.

The pace of his job had him starting to feel like an old man himself when he left the paper at age 57.

"Everything had been job, job, job, job," he says. "I'm learning to put the brakes on the fast lane. Maybe I still spend a little too much time in the clubs. That whole crowd out there in the rock scene can get you into trouble. I have to take care of myself. I have to watch it."

We meet for lunch in Porter Square at Andy's Diner, a breakfast-served-all-day place where it would be hard to get into trouble. Bono is on another continent, and the writer is talking about the gentle pace of freelancing reviews and travel pieces, doing liner notes and biographies for recording covers. "The work I do now is for pleasure," he says.

"RETIREMENT IS ABOUT BALANCE," says the garden writer. "It's about figuring out what's important."

She decided to leave the paper because her husband was being treated for a brain tumor — he has since recovered. "I thought, 'Life is short.' I was looking at my husband's possible death and I thought of all those years gone and eaten up by deadlines. I felt the clock running out. When you work at the *Globe*, that's all you have time to do."

She has been freelancing for the paper, has written a book, is in demand as a speaker, and has found that living her old life part-time is a nice pace. "It's like skating on the surface of the *Globe*. It's just enough."

She has had both knees replaced since leaving the paper, and she does a lot of physical therapy and gym work. When we meet at a Japanese restaurant in East Milton Square, she is about to go to California for a month and plans to take classes at a YMCA that are geared toward people over age 60.

"You have to keep working at it," she says. "You have to keep moving."

The economy is a worry, but she repeats that the key is balance. "The balance is between the voice that says, 'Don't spend the money. You can't afford it,' and the one that says, 'Carpe diem!'"

A friend of hers is dying of cancer and wants to go to Barcelona because they traveled there once before. "So I balance it out. I look at the budget. No, I don't need HBO. But, yes, I'm going to Barcelona with my girlfriend. It will probably be our last trip together."

Before she left the *Globe*, she made a list of 30 or 40 things she'd do in retirement, and they included writing a novel, writing a family history, and starting a commune for aging hippies. When she retired, she ignored the list, fell into freelancing, and kept gardening.

"Thinking about what you'll do in retirement is like having a conversation with your fiancé about marriage," she says. "You ask, 'How many children will we have?' or 'Would you relocate if I got another job?' You go through the list, think you have the answers, and then you get married and don't do any of those things. Life goes on. But it's good to have had the conversation."

It is always good to have the conversation, and I am glad to have had all these and more. Coming home from what usually turned into an afternoon of lunch, I feel lucky to know these interesting souls and to hear echoes of my own experience in their words. They surprise me, inspire me, and make me laugh. Some people made me laugh so much telling old *Globe* stories that I forgot to take notes and so couldn't include them here.

Several of these retirement conversations are the first time a colleague and I have ever really talked beyond exchanging "Hi, how are ya" in the hall. Other times, we are reconnecting after years of being on different tracks.

When I was working full-time at the *Globe*, work was not the place for long sit-downs and chats from the heart. A leisurely lunch in a restaurant for pleasure rather than business was a rarity at the newspaper, where it was referred to as "an out-of-building experience." People grabbed salads in the *Globe* cafeteria and often ate them at their desks. In addition to time constraints, there were those walls, physical and psychological, erected between people. He or she was in The Big Office and seemed unapproachable. He or she was always on the phone, on the run, too intense to stop. He or she might have told someone who shouldn't know about a blurted-out insecurity, fear, or desire. Work was about being tough, taking it, getting it done, impressing the hierarchy and the underlings.

Retirement is the great leveler. We can be who we are. We can embrace the tearing down of walls, real and imagined. There is time to eat slowly, have seconds, and share the human journey. It's all one big out-of-building experience now.

→ CHAPTER 19 ←

Not the Conclusion

If the last chapter of a book is supposed to wrap things up neatly and send readers on their way with something definitive, I'm in trouble. The only thing I know for sure about retirement is that it's a lot like what a teacher in a writing class said about creating fiction: "You have to learn to live with confusion, to just go with it even though you have no idea what's about to happen next."

Retirement is a lot like jazz that way. It can be wild and wailing one minute as it takes the melody into outer space, then come back down to earth, mellow and familiar the next. All of life can feel that way, actually, and the only difference now is that I'm living it older and unemployed.

Retirement/life/the-great-Whatever is messy and contradictory, and probably the easiest way to get a grip on it is to not grip too tightly, or to insist on forming a conclusion about the concert while the music is still playing. The best I can do for summation right now is that I'm hearing all the notes, sometimes all at once, and relishing the show even when it makes me nervous.

Most of the questions, insecurities, fears, hopes, and struggles making their demands in this phase of life will keep on demanding. One day, in the next phase, whatever that may be, they could be resolved, packed away, or traded in for new demands. But for now, they're not going anywhere except with me. On good days, I'll look at them and say, "Oh, yeah, you again. I can get through this because I'm learning to live with confusion." On bad days, I may call the physiatrist.

When I first retired, I felt like a plucked chicken in a new barnyard. Now I'm a plucked chicken in more familiar space. It could be that I'm growing a new set of feathers, but it's too early to tell what they'll look like.

I don't have grand plans. Not yet. No vision to climb Mount Everest, join the Peace Corps, or fly a plane. Today I have small plans to keep writing, tend the garden, tend the mind and keep it open, tend to friends, and to be spontaneous when one of them invites me to a lecture on mosquitoes just because it sounds interesting.

The talk was titled, "My Life as a Mosquito: Narrative, Disease, and Agro-Ecology in a Malaria Landscape." The lecturer was James McCann, a history professor at Boston University, and as part of his presentation, he did a terrific first-person narrative as an insect. Sitting in the seminar room on a Friday afternoon, hearing about Africa and crops and epidemics, I thought: this is cool because it has absolutely nothing to do with anything in my life and it's fascinating.

I thought of the Liza Minelli song, "Yes" with its message to be open to the moment and to not weigh contingencies so heavily that they lead to "No."

Breakfast at 8:00 A.M. in Boston? Sure. Spur-of-the-moment Freedom Trail tour with my niece and her boyfriend? Absolutely. A long phone conversation with a childhood friend even though I have to pack for a trip, do laundry, and pay bills? Of course. Want to drive down to Providence to see the Culinary Arts Museum? Never heard of it, but all the more reason to go. Concert in the park? I'm there. A reunion in Ohio with my old college roommate? Yes. Yes!

I dash this way and that, following no straight lines to a clear goal, probably looking like a headless chicken at times as well as a plucked one. I start out to read the newspaper, see an interesting interview with an author, go to the computer to e-mail the link to the writing group, go to the bookcase to check the short-story anthologies to see whether I've got anything by that author, decide to go to the bookstore to find her work, remember the dry cleaning to be picked up on the way, and don't get back to the newspaper until it's time for dinner, which I make while reading the front page.

On good days, this is energizing and freeing. On bad days, it feels like attention deficit–hyperactivity disorder.

Am I drifting? That's another unanswered question that is going with me into the next phase, along with: Is it okay to drift? I don't understand the concept of leisure time yet because being busy doesn't feel like leisure, and what I'm busy with doesn't feel like the old job. I'm a tweener and figuring out what that means.

"I'll never retire," friends have said proudly, and one has said she doesn't "believe" in retirement, as though being retired is like Santa Claus or the Tooth Fairy. When I've asked some people if they plan to retire, they have taken the question as an insult, as though this is a suggestion to head for the pasture. It's not. There is no pasture out here, folks. It's more like an airport. All kinds of aircraft going all kinds of places, offering boundless choices and possibilities. The world awaits. The traveler just has to decide where he or she is going, or not going, be aware of sudden wind shifts, and set no itinerary in cement.

Sometimes I think I'm sure about what I don't want. No committee work, no senior bus tours, no self-righteous political movements, no okra, no Jane Austen. But then I remember "Yes." I remember a piece of Joseph Campbell's wisdom: "We must be willing to get rid of the life we've planned, so as to have the life that is waiting for us."

And what would that be, that life that is waiting? Finding it requires not so much running around as times of quiet, meditation, and patience — which I am often lacking. To calm the confusion, I read the Psalms and the words of Jesus, Lao-tzu, Rumi, Emerson, Mary Baker Eddy, the Dalai Lama, Sister Joan Chittister, and Joan Borysenko.

I go to a women's retreat on an island in Maine in August and find calm in our church service by the sea on Sunday morning, in the walks to the lighthouse, and in my tent on the shore, where I can hear the ocean waves. I find peace in the reunion with people who can laugh through four days without running water or electricity.

The first day, I stumble over rocks and logs, feel discombobulated getting in and out of the tent on all fours, forget to zip the flap to keep the bugs out, and head down to dinner around the big picnic table without my flashlight, forgetting that the walk back after dinner will be in darkness except for the stars.

By the next day, I find my feet and start to walk confidently where there are no paths. I remember to carry spare flashlight batteries. I can work the cranky cistern spigot and hose to put rainwater in the washbasin. I sit in the outhouse, look out at the birds, and don't feel strange. I do the breaststroke in the icy ocean that at first had seemed too cold for wading. I swim to shore and the island welcomes me back. It and I just needed time to adjust.

Groping along life's paths, waiting to adjust, takes more time. How much time depends on the person, the path, the feet, and where the flashlight is pointed. Learning how to be retired is a journey not unlike growing up. Is a human being ever totally *there*, all grown up and complete? Not really, because there is always more to learn. There is no one "right" way to make the trip. No simple answer. No conclusion, because people are in transition as long as they're alive.

I walk forward, not quite sorting it out, knowing, as it says in Ecclesiastes, that there is a season for all things, and a time for every purpose under heaven. I remember the words of Teddy Roosevelt, too, and not just "Bully!" although that's as good as "Yes." I'm thinking of this one: "Do what you can, where you are, with what you have."

And then? Move on and do it again.

Where am I going? Somewhere. Somewhere interesting. We'll see.

Acknowledgments

Writing is a lonely trade but publishing needs a crowd. I was lucky to have had a great group of wise, caring, fun people lending their time and talent to this project.

Thank you to:

+ Colleen Mohyde who believed in the book from the first phone conversation and whose enthusiasm kept me at the task.

+ Sharon Cloud Hogan for her enthusiasm, careful editing, insight, and patience dealing with a low-tech author.

+ Janis Owens, who connected with the words and gave them visual life in cover art and interior design.

+ The *Boston Globe* colleagues who shared their retirement stories and shared all those years with me at the newspaper. Special thanks to Jan Shepherd for moral support and good talks at lunch.

+ The members of the Barnes & Noble writing group who helped shape early drafts. I particularly appreciate the final draft proofreading by Ray Anderson, Art Burdett, Carol Chubb, Jenn Harris, Alan Kennedy, and Virginia Young.

✦ Jean Pratt, my cheerleader, and 91-year-old girlfriend.

✦ Jean's daughter, Joanna, and son-in-law, Steve Samuels, who spent a weekend reading the book and laughing in the right places. Jean's daughter, Judith, for being my writing friend since the days when our typing table was a trunk in a fifth-floor walk-up apartment in New York City.

✦ John Stobierski, my love, who said it was time to leave the newspaper and try something new — and who believed I could.

Breinigsville, PA USA
31 March 2011
258890BV00001B/158/P